THE NATURE
OF MATTER

PHYSICS IN ACTION

Energy

Forces and Motion

The Nature of Matter

Planets, Stars, and Galaxies

Processes That Shape the Earth

PHYSICS in ACTION

THE NATURE OF MATTER

Daniel T. Larson

Series Editor
David G. Haase

CHELSEA HOUSE
PUBLISHERS
An imprint of Infobase Publishing

The Nature of Matter

Chelsea House
An imprint of Infobase Publishing
132 West 31st Street
New York NY 10001

Library of Congress Cataloging-in-Publication Data
Larson, Daniel.
   The Nature of matter / Daniel T. Larson.
     p. cm. — (Physics in action)
   Includes bibliographical references and index.
   ISBN-13: 978-0-7910-8929-3 (hardcover)
   ISBN-10: 0-7910-8929-0 (hardcover)
  1. Matter. I. Title. II. Series.
   QC171.2.L385 2007
   530—dc22   2007010159

Chelsea House books are available at special discounts when purchased in bulk quantities for businesses, associations, institutions, or sales promotions. Please call our Special Sales Department in New York at (212) 967-8800 or (800) 322-8755.

You can find Chelsea House on the World Wide Web at http://www.chelseahouse.com

Text design by James Scotto-Lavino
Cover design by Takeshi Takahashi

Printed in the United States of America

Bang NMSG 10 9 8 7 6 5 4 3 2 1

This book is printed on acid-free paper.

All links and Web addresses were checked and verified to be correct at the time of publication. Because of the dynamic nature of the Web, some addresses and links may have changed since publication and may no longer be valid.

CONTENTS

1   Inner Space 7

2   The Rise of the Atom 16

3   Organizing Atoms 28

4   The Periodic Table of the Elements 34

5   Chemical Bonds 46

6   Radioactivity 63

7   Nuclear Energy 75

8   Elementary Particle Physics 84

Glossary. 93

Bibliography 98

Further Reading 99

Index 101

CHAPTER 1

Inner Space

"PLEASE PLACE YOUR SEAT BACKS AND TRAY TABLES IN THEIR full upright and locked positions. The Inner Space ship is about to depart." Imagine that you are onboard a special ship that doesn't fly fast or far, but rather *shrinks*. This ship won't help you visit your aunt in Nebraska, but it will help you learn about the basic building blocks of the world.

Today the Inner Space ship is going to explore a glass of water. You start out gazing at a full glass sitting on the table. It is a normal glass that could fit easily in your hand. But as the engines on the ship engage, you feel yourself shrinking and watch the glass of water growing. Pretty soon the glass is as big as a building, and your ship moves inside it. As you keep shrinking, the glass keeps growing, but all you can see around you is water. You continue shrinking, and eventually the water changes from looking smooth and seamless to having small lumps. Those lumps grow, and you can see that they are water molecules. These **molecules** are the smallest pieces of water that still have the properties of water. They are bumping around each other in a random way. Your trip so far is summarized in the top part of Figure 1.1.

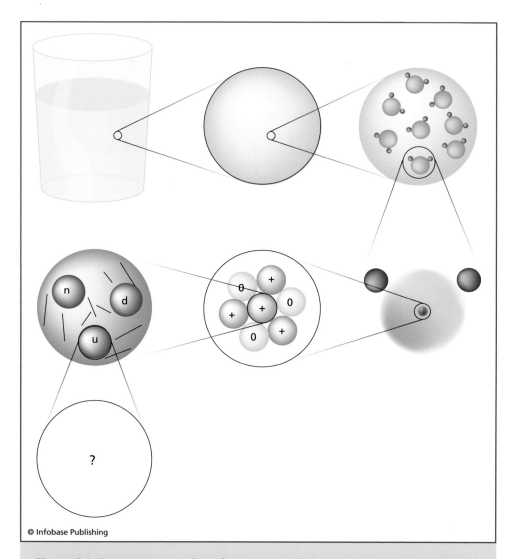

Figure 1.1 *Zooming in on a glass of water, you will start to see the individual water molecules made up of atoms (top right). Zooming in on a molecule shows the atoms with a nucleus that is made up of protons and neutrons (middle center). Those protons and neutrons are each made up of three quarks (middle left). Whether the quarks are made up of something else is still an open question.*

As your ship continues to shrink, the water molecules begin to appear larger, and you can see that they are each composed of three smaller lumps stuck together, one big one in the middle with two smaller lumps attached almost like Mickey-Mouse ears. These three parts of the water molecule are called **atoms**. Your ship continues to shrink and zooms in on the largest lump in the water molecule, an oxygen atom. The oxygen atom appears to be a fuzzy sphere, and as you get closer and closer you see that the fuzziness is mostly caused by **electrons**, negatively charged particles that make up the fuzzy sphere but are each much smaller than the sphere itself. As you zoom in on the oxygen atom and enter the electron cloud, all you see is the occasional electron whizzing by, but most of the rest of the time there is just empty space. Undaunted, your ship continues to shrink, and eventually you see a small speck growing larger and larger. That speck is the atomic **nucleus**, the core of the oxygen atom that contains most of its mass. As the nucleus grows larger, you start to see that it, too, is made up of smaller pieces that are tightly bound together. Those smaller pieces are of two types, **protons**, which carry positive charge, and **neutrons**, which do not carry any electrical charge. Zooming in even closer, you enter a proton or neutron and discover that it is itself composed of 3 smaller particles called **quarks**. You pick out one of the quarks and start to zoom in on it and you see . . . nothing yet. Unfortunately, scientists have not yet been able to look close enough at quarks to explore whether they are also made up of some smaller particle. But the search continues to find the smallest building blocks of the universe.

Suddenly the seat belt sign is illuminated and you are instructed to prepare for landing. You are back at your normal size, sitting in your chair and gazing at the glass of water. Looking around you see many different types of matter. You might see wood, stone, plastic, cloth, air, or water. These materials all seem so different from each other. Do they have anything in common? One way to try to answer this question is to compare the smallest parts that make up an object. This investigational approach is called **reductionism**. In this book, we will seek to find the building blocks that are common to all of these various materials.

SMALLER AND SMALLER CONSTITUENTS

Molecules

Recall your imaginary trip zooming in on a glass of water. At first, all you could see when magnifying the water was more water. If you pour out half of the water in the glass, you would just have less water. If you pour out half of the remaining water, you still just have a smaller quantity of water. But if you keep pouring out half of the remaining water, you would eventually wind up with a sample containing the smallest piece of water that can still be called water, namely, a water molecule. Water molecules are indescribably tiny. In a glass of water there are roughly 8 trillion trillion water molecules.

Many other substances are also made up of molecules. The air we breathe consists mostly of nitrogen gas molecules, with some oxygen and carbon dioxide molecules mixed in. Our bodies are full of specialized molecules. Hemoglobin carries oxygen in our bloodstream. The blueprints for constructing new cells are contained in large, complex molecules called DNA. But molecules are not the smallest constituents of matter.

Atoms

If you look even closer at a molecule, you will see that it is made up of smaller lumps called atoms. Each molecule is made up of a specific collection of atoms, some big and some small. If you were to replace one of the atoms in a molecule with a different one, you would have a different molecule. There are 92 different kinds of atoms that occur naturally in the world. Also, more than 20 heavier atoms have been produced artificially in the laboratory. At first, 112 different atoms may sound like a lot, but consider how many different kinds of material you can think of. There are probably more than 100 different kinds of cloth alone, not to mention thousands of different types of rock, and numerous chemicals inside your body. It is amazing that all these different materials are each made up of their own distinct molecules, but those millions of different molecules are made from about 100 atomic building blocks. It is as if there were only 100 types of Lego pieces from which you could build the entire universe.

Electrons, Protons, and Neutrons

The universe is more amazing still! If you look closer at each of the different known atoms, you will see that they are all quite similar. They are all made of a very small but heavy and positively charged nucleus, surrounded by tiny negatively charged electrons. The nucleus is more than 10,000 times smaller than the atom as a whole, but if you zoom in on the nucleus, you would see that it is also made up of smaller pieces called protons and neutrons.

Quarks

Look closer at protons and neutrons . . . there is something smaller inside them also. The proton and neutron are each made up of two types of quarks, playfully called the "up quark" and the "down quark." The proton is made of two up quarks and one down quark, whereas the neutron is made of two down quarks and one up quark.

Something Smaller?

Can we keep going, always finding smaller and smaller components? So far, no matter how closely we look at the quarks they do not seem to have any smaller pieces. Similarly, the electron doesn't have any smaller components, as far as we can tell. We call particles that cannot be divided **elementary particles**. But such a term is never set in stone. For a time people thought atoms were elementary particles, but with increasingly sophisticated scientific instruments, they were able to look closer at atoms and discover that they were made of electrons, protons, and neutrons. It is possible that quarks and electrons are not elementary, but are made up of still smaller particles that are too small for us to detect.

Indeed, many scientists are trying very hard to find ever smaller constituents of matter. It's an exciting quest to find the most fundamental building blocks of all matter.

FOUR FORCES

Our world not only has "stuff" in it, but that stuff interacts with other stuff through what we call **forces**. We are surrounded by things happening: balls bouncing, apples falling from trees, fireworks exploding, water freezing. Each of these events is the result of forces between objects. Amazingly, all of nature can be explained by the actions of four fundamental forces: gravity, electromagnetism, the weak nuclear force, and the strong nuclear force. They are summarized in Table 1.1.

TABLE 1.1 The Four Fundamental Forces

NAME	PARTICLES AFFECTED	EFFECTS
Gravity	All massive particles and objects	Objects falling to the ground; holding people to the Earth; orbits of the planets
Electromagnetism	All electrically charged particles (including electrons and protons)	Electricity; lightning; magnets; light; holding atoms together in solids
Weak Nuclear Force	Electrons, protons, neutrons, neutrinos	Radioactivity
Strong Nuclear Force	Protons and neutrons	Holding atomic nuclei together; energy released in nuclear reactors and nuclear bombs

Gravity

Gravity is the most obvious force in your everyday life. When you drop something, gravity pulls it to the ground. Isaac Newton made the wonderful discovery that the force of gravity that makes the apple fall to the ground is also responsible for the orbit of the Moon around the Earth and the Earth around the Sun. On the microscopic level, however, gravity is extremely weak. It doesn't play any role in the interactions between atoms and molecules, and won't concern us much in this book.

Electromagnetism

Electromagnetism is the name of the force responsible for the attraction between opposite electrical charges and the repulsion of identical charges. It is also responsible for pulling a compass needle to point north. While gravity is what pulls you from a tree to the ground, it is the electromagnetic force that actually keeps you from falling through the floor. The electromagnetic force holds electrons in atoms and holds atoms together in molecules. Thus, electromagnetism is the most important force for understanding chemical reactions and the differences between different types of matter. Electromagnetism is the force behind the atoms and bonding discussed in Chapters 2 to 5.

The Weak and Strong Nuclear Forces

There are two more forces that are not easy to see in everyday life, because they are most important for the tiny nucleus inside of atoms. These two forces have very unimaginative names. The first is the **weak nuclear force,** which is responsible for a form of radioactivity called **beta decay**. Radioactivity is important for technological applications and safety, and we will discuss it in more detail in Chapter 6. The second is the **strong nuclear force,** which is responsible for holding the protons and neutrons together inside the nucleus. This force is very important for understanding nuclear interactions and is the force behind nuclear power and nuclear weapons. These two fundamental forces will be discussed in Chapters 7 and 8.

The Size of an Atom and Its Nucleus

Here is a simple exercise to give you a sense of the size of an atom and its nucleus. Start with a normal 8.5" × 11" piece of paper. Find the halfway point on the longer side and cut it in half. Now take one of those halves and cut it in half again on the same side. Again, take one of the remaining halves, now a quarter of the original sheet of paper, and cut it in half a third time. You can keep doing this, cutting the remaining piece of paper in half, all on the same side. If you are really careful you might be able to do this ten times. Now compare what you have left to a full sheet of paper. After the tenth "halving" of the paper, the remaining really thin slice is about 1,000 times smaller than the size of the original paper.

This next part you won't be able to do with normal scissors and paper. Imagine taking that final really thin strip of paper and doing the same procedure again, cutting it in half ten times. Then take the result and imagine cutting it in half *another* ten times. After that, the width of the final sheet of paper would be about the size of a molecule or atom. It is nearly impossible to imagine something that small. If you can imagine taking that atom and cutting it in half ten times in a row, however, you would be left with something that is nearly 100 times *larger* than the average atomic nucleus. Atoms really are tiny, and nuclei are much smaller still.

MATERIAL IN OUR WORLD

When you get down to the sub-sub-microscopic level, our world appears to be relatively simple. At the most fundamental level, every object in the universe is made up of two types of constituents: quarks and electrons. These two types of particles interact through only four forces: gravity, electromagnetism, and the weak and strong nuclear forces. But the objects we encounter every day are even simpler. All of the physical and chemical interactions between us and the materials surrounding us are due to the electromagnetic interactions of atomic electrons. It is truly amazing that these few ingredients are enough to make up the multitude of different rocks, plants, and animals that surround us.

CHAPTER 2

The Rise of the Atom

Everyone is familiar with the multitude of substances that surround us: air, dirt, wood, water, cloth, metal, plastic, paper. . . . The list could go on for many pages. But did you ever think to wonder *why* there are so many types of "stuff"?

Certainly many ancient peoples wondered about all the stuff surrounding them, but the ancient Greeks are the earliest people whose ideas on this topic have been preserved to the present day. Before 500 B.C., several philosophers in the Greek city of Miletus had come up with ideas about the fundamental components of the world. Thales thought everything in the world was composed of water, whereas Anaximines thought that air was the primary substance. About 200 years later in the town of Abdera, Democritus (460–370 B.C.) popularized the concept of atoms, small particles of different types that made up everything material. But at the same time, the philosopher Plato advocated the competing idea that everything was made up of four basic substances: air, earth, fire, and water. These conclusions were formed by philosophers, who studied these ideas by thinking about them. It wasn't until scientists started doing actual experiments that they discovered, in the early 1800s, that it was Democritus and his atoms that were nearer the truth.

REVERSE BAKING

How would you go about answering the question "What is the world made of?" It turns out to be kind of like baking, but in reverse. If you eat a wonderful dessert you might ask the chef for the recipe. The recipe is a list of ingredients and instructions that tell you how to make the dessert. But what if you had only the dessert and nobody to give you the recipe? That is the situation the scientists of the 1700s faced. They wanted to know the recipe for the different materials they found around them, but there was nobody to ask. So they had to start doing experiments to take the substances apart and determine their basic components. Imagine trying to take a cake apart to determine its ingredients. By dissolving, heating, boiling, and mixing with other substances you could eventually determine that the cake was made up of flour, sugar, salt, butter, and so on. This was exactly what chemists like Antoine Lavoisier (1743–1794) spent their time doing, trying to find the basic ingredients in material like gunpowder or diamonds.

We know what the ingredients in a dessert are likely to be, namely, the items commonly found in a kitchen. But what are the ingredients Lavoisier was looking for? Lavoisier's goal was to take a complicated substance like gunpowder and determine which chemical elements made it up. Most substances can be separated into several simpler substances. Elements, however, are the substances that, try as you might, cannot be broken up into anything more fundamental using the methods of chemistry. For instance, the air in the room can be separated into several types of gases, mostly nitrogen and oxygen, with some water vapor mixed in. By putting an electric current through water, it can be separated into hydrogen and oxygen gases. But try as you might, the hydrogen gas can't be separated into any other substances. Hydrogen, nitrogen, and oxygen are examples of **elements**, the basic ingredients out of which the complex substances around us are built.

Antoine and Marie-Anne Lavoisier

The experiments of Antoine and Marie-Anne Lavoisier (Figure 2.1) were instrumental in making the study of matter and chemicals much more scientific. Antoine was the son of a wealthy French lawyer and received a first-rate education. Despite his interest in science, he made an important business move and purchased a share in the Ferme Générale, an agency that collected taxes for the government. This had positive and negative consequences. The income from this venture helped provide Antoine with enough money so that he could dedicate much of his time to chemistry experiments.

Figure 2.1 *Antoine and Marie-Anne Lavoisier worked together closely in the search for the basic ingredients in material like gunpowder or diamonds.*

One of Lavoisier's partners in the Ferme had a daughter named Marie-Anne Pierrette, whom Lavoisier married despite the fact that she was only 14 at the time and he was 28, twice her age. They got along splendidly, however, and Marie-Anne worked alongside Antoine doing chemistry research. Unfortunately, Antoine's affiliation with the Ferme made him very unpopular with some members of the French Revolution and led to his death at the guillotine on May 8, 1794.

Elements are basic ingredients that can be put together to make a **compound**. One example of a compound is sugar, which is composed of the elements carbon, hydrogen, and oxygen. Those three elements can combine in a very specific way to make sugar. If you then combine the sugar with some salt, flour, and other ingredients you will obtain a mixture. The mixture has molecules of many different types all jumbled together. By adding liquid ingredients and heating the mixture you can cause **chemical reactions** to take place. During chemical reactions some of the elements separate from each other and reassemble in a different form. If you are lucky, the result will taste very good, and you can also call it a dessert.

Lavoisier was interested in determining which elements were contained in gunpowder and other various substances. But deeper questions about the elements still remained. What is an element, really? Are elements made up of anything smaller?

JOHN DALTON

John Dalton was not the first person since Democritus to think about atoms. His experiments with gases, however, provided some of the data that got people to accept the atomic hypothesis.

Dalton was born in 1766 in England. His early education was haphazard, but he eventually became a professor at New College in Manchester, and while there he became fascinated with the atmosphere. During his studies he explored the properties of gases, and in particular the interesting result that related materials seemed to be formed out of more basic substances in fixed proportions. For example, he observed that the ratio of hydrogen to carbon in methane gas was exactly twice the ratio of hydrogen to carbon in ethylene gas. This observation could be neatly explained if the carbon and hydrogen, and all other elements, came in small indivisible bundles called atoms.

Dalton surmised that all elements were made of such atoms, but he didn't know what these minute atoms might be. He envisioned them to be tiny solids surrounded by heat energy. This turns out not to be a very accurate picture of an atom. Nevertheless, even though the details were wrong Dalton was on the right track. The idea that atoms were the basic units of substance was very useful for understanding chemical compounds and quickly caught on.

MODERN ATOMIC MODELS

Scientific Explanations

Science is done by making educated guesses about how the world works and then testing those guesses by doing experiments. Such an educated guess is called a hypothesis. If a hypothesis correctly explains all the experiments anyone can think of, then scientists start to trust it and it can get elevated to the status of a theory or model. A model that correctly explains the results of some experiments, however, might turn out to fail once better experiments are done. Often the model is revised and improved to take into account the new results. This new model might work for quite a long time, but often some new, more detailed experiments will come along and show that the old model is not quite right and needs yet more revision. Thus, there is a constant dialogue between the predictions of models and experimental results.

Pudding or Muffin, Anyone?

Experiments in the late 1800s uncovered many mysterious rays being emitted by different substances. Some of the rays turned out to be associated with radioactivity, which we will examine in detail in Chapter 6. Another kind of ray, called a **cathode ray**, was emitted when a high voltage was applied to a metal. These rays could be bent by a magnetic field, so it was clear they were electrically charged. In 1897, J.J. Thomson suggested that these rays were actually negatively charged particles. By measuring the ratio of their charge and mass he concluded that the particles must be much smaller than the smallest atoms known. He thus correctly identified the electron. Because the electron appeared to be coming out of the individual atoms, its existence contradicted Dalton's view that atoms were indivisible. Atoms surely existed, but they were composed of smaller pieces.

Early in the 1900s, there was speculation about how the electrons fit inside atoms. Since they were so light, there either had to be very many of them or something else had to account for most of the mass of heavy atoms like gold. Also, the electrons were negatively charged, which meant that there had to be positive charges somewhere so that together they could form neutral atoms. In 1904, Thomson described a model of the atom that was playfully called the **plum pudding model**, because back then plum puddings were something people were familiar with. Nowadays, it would more likely be called the "raisin muffin model." The idea was that the small, negatively charged electrons were stuck in a big, heavy blob of positively charged dough, much like the plums in a pudding or the raisins in a muffin, as shown in Figure 2.2. This model explained why the particles in the cathode rays were always negatively charged. A high voltage could pop the small, light electrons out of the atom but couldn't move the heavy positive dough surrounding them. Thomson's model was a good start, but it couldn't explain the results of later experiments.

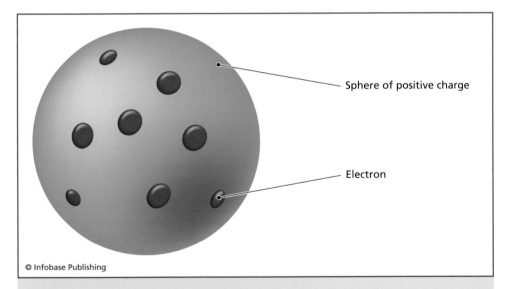

© Infobase Publishing

Figure 2.2 *The plum pudding or raisin muffin model of the atom described by J.J. Thomson. In this model, small, negative electrons are stuck like plums or raisins in a positively charged dough.*

The Rutherford Model

In 1911, Ernest Rutherford and his students in England conducted a wonderful experiment where they sent a beam of **alpha particles** into a thin sheet of gold foil and watched where the alpha particles came out. Alpha particles were known to be helium atoms without their electrons, which means they are positive particles. Most of the alpha particles went straight through the gold foil, only slightly deflected by collisions within the foil. The surprising discovery, however, was that a small number of alpha particles came bouncing back, almost as if they had hit a solid wall. In order to account for this strange behavior, Rutherford devised a new model of the atom. Instead of a uniform dough of positive charge with small negative electrons (raisins) embedded in it, Rutherford suggested that all of the positive charge and most of the mass was concentrated in a small, central nucleus, and that the rest of the atom was mostly empty space with the tiny electrons in some type of orbit around the nucleus. Based on his experimental data, Rutherford determined that the nucleus was about 10,000 times smaller than the atom itself. This picture of the atom is called the **Rutherford model**, but could also be more descriptively called the **solar system model**, because the electrons orbit around the positive nucleus in much the same way that the planets orbit around the sun.

A cartoon image of this model of the atom is shown in Figure 2.3. In the solar system model, the very light electrons (planets) would be much easier to knock out of their orbits than the massive nucleus (sun). Thus, it still explained the earlier discoveries of Thomson that the negative particles could escape the atom. But in addition, the solar system model could explain Rutherford's discovery about alpha particles. Most of the time alpha particles could fly right through the atoms without being disturbed, but every once in a while, when they headed right for a nucleus, they would be deflected backwards by the electric repulsion of like charges. This new Rutherford (or solar system) model improved upon the plum pudding (or raisin muffin) model, and was quickly adopted.

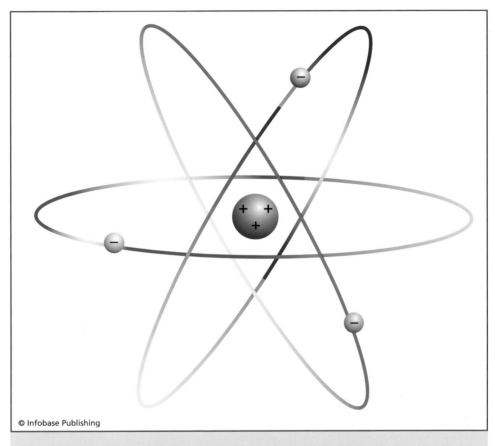

© Infobase Publishing

Figure 2.3 *In the Rutherford or solar system model of the atom, a small, positively charged nucleus is orbited by even smaller negatively charged electrons.*

The Bohr Model

In 1913, Niels Bohr made some bold suggestions that resulted in significant improvements in the solar system model. Since the 1890s, scientists had known that different atoms could only absorb and emit certain colors of light. However, the formula specifying the colors had only been determined empirically—that is, by educated guessing. Nobody could derive the formula from the known principles of physics. In 1905, Albert Einstein suggested that light came in small packets called **photons** and that the amount of energy in each photon was given by the product of the frequency of the light and Planck's constant, h, a fundamental constant of nature. Since the color of light is determined by its frequency, Einstein's idea of photons connected the specific colors emitted by atoms to specific amounts of energy. Bohr used this connection to devise a model of the atom that explained these bundles of energy.

Bohr's model of the atom was based on the structure of the solar system model. In the middle of the atom was the heavy, positively charged nucleus that Rutherford had discovered, and it was still orbited by tiny electrons. Bohr, however, suggested that those electrons couldn't orbit in just any old fashion but could only travel in certain, specific orbits. When an electron moved from one of these allowed orbits to another, it gave off a photon of light carrying an amount of energy equal to the difference between the energies of the initial allowed orbit and the final allowed orbit. Since there were only certain allowed orbits, there were specific sets of allowed transitions corresponding to the colors of light emitted by the atom. This model, shown in Figure 2.4, worked quite well, because it incorporated the electron and nucleus discovered by Thomson and Rutherford, and also accounted for the observed discrete amounts of energy emitted by atoms, matching the formula discovered more than 20 years earlier. The Bohr model was thus a more sophisticated version of the solar system model and allowed scientists to predict the colors of light given off by atoms. It also is not a bad basic image to have in your head when thinking about atoms. Later experiments, however, showed that despite its successes, even Bohr's model of the atom wasn't quite right either.

Quantum Mechanics

The many strange observations about atoms and light made in the early 1900s were finally put together in the framework of quantum mechanics by 1927. Within quantum mechanics, the model of the atom was modified yet again. There is still a heavy nucleus, but the electron doesn't really orbit as Bohr described it. Rather it is smeared out within a specific energy level or **orbital** (Figure 2.5).

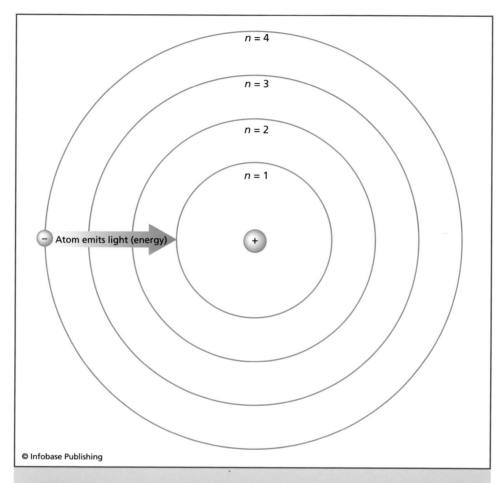

n = 4

n = 3

n = 2

n = 1

− Atom emits light (energy)   +

Figure 2.4 *In the Bohr model of the atom, the negative electrons orbit the positively charged nucleus, but they can only occupy specific energy levels. When the electron moves between energy levels, light (energy) is either emitted or absorbed.*

Nevertheless, the energy levels predicted by Bohr's model still remained, with small corrections.

Scientists strive to understand even the smallest details. More precise measurements of atoms showed that the predictions from quantum mechanics were not quite right. A newer, grander theory called quantum electrodynamics (QED) was developed to describe the energy levels of atoms to great precision. So far there haven't been any experiments that disagree with QED, and it remains as one of the most successful theories of physics. Who knows, however, what will happen in the future, as experiments grow ever more precise? It is entirely possible that some ultra-precise experiment will measure atomic properties that disagree with the predictions from QED, requiring more refinement or another new model to more accurately describe the atom. Any new model of the atom, however, must incorporate all the previous successes of QED before it can be taken seriously.

Bohr's Hydrogen Atom

Bohr's model of the atom was a leap forward because it gave a quantitative description of the atom's structure. For the hydrogen atom, Bohr could calculate the values of the energy levels that could be occupied by the electron. It turns out that those energy levels can be labeled by a number n, the **principal quantum number**. The formula for the energy levels in the hydrogen atom is:

$$E_n = -(13.6 \text{ eV})/n^2$$

The lowest energy state, or ground state, has $n = 1$, which corresponds to an energy of $E_1 = -13.6$ eV. (An eV or electron-volt is a very small unit of energy; 1 electron-volt is equal to 1.6×10^{-19} joules.) The first excited state has $n = 2$ and energy $E_2 = -13.6/2^2$ eV $= -3.4$ eV. Furthermore, Bohr's model predicted that the energy emitted by an atom would come in specific amounts corresponding to the differences between energy levels. For example, if an electron jumps from the first excited state down to the ground state it would emit a photon of light with energy $E_2 - E_1 = (-3.4 \text{ eV}) - (-13.6 \text{ eV}) = 10.2$ eV. These predictions for the emitted photons matched the results that had been observed, giving strong support to the Bohr model.

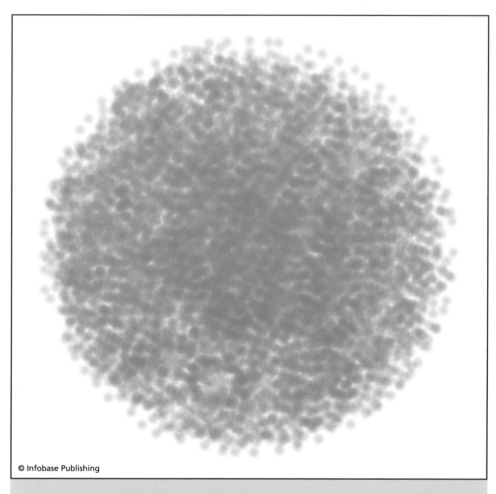

Figure 2.5 *The quantum model of the atom, where the electrons do not follow specific paths around the nucleus but instead are smeared out within each energy level.*

Even though Bohr's model of the atom was shown to be incomplete, it still explains the basic properties of atoms well enough to understand the interactions between atoms that are important for building molecules and compounds and understanding the general properties of different forms of matter.

CHAPTER 3

Organizing Atoms

EVER SINCE THE TIME OF RUTHERFORD, WE HAVE KNOWN that atoms consist of a tiny, massive, positively charged nucleus surrounded by a distant cloud of negatively charged electrons. In 1930, James Chadwick explained the results of several experiments by postulating a neutral particle, the neutron, that should be found in the nucleus. The neutron has nearly the same mass as a proton, about 1.67×10^{-27} kg. In contrast, electrons weigh only 9.11×10^{-31} kg, nearly 2,000 times less. To get a feel for how big a difference that is, imagine if we enlarged an electron so that it weighed 1 pound (0.45 kg). Then a similarly enlarged proton or neutron would weigh almost a ton (907 kg).

So how are all the different atoms organized? We now know that all atoms are made up of protons, neutrons, and electrons in various combinations. But long before anybody knew about those subatomic particles, scientists like Antoine Lavoisier knew that there were certain pure types of material called elements, and the scientists gave names to many of those elements. When discussing atoms, we still use those historical names. Now that we know about protons, neutrons, and electrons, however, we also use numbers to describe different atoms.

ATOMIC NUMBER

Every element is made up of atoms that all have the same number of protons in their nucleus. Hydrogen atoms all have one proton, helium atoms have two, and lithium atoms have three protons. The number of protons in the nucleus is called the **atomic number**. Thus, all atoms with the same atomic number have the same name. The atomic number is usually called Z for short. For example, since an atom of gold has 79 protons, we would say that gold has Z = 79, which means that the atomic number of gold is 79. In contrast, Z = 1 refers to hydrogen and Z = 3 indicates lithium. Each element's name has an abbreviation or representation of one or two letters called the **chemical symbol**. The symbol for hydrogen is H; for helium, it is He. Some symbols, however, are not as obvious. For example, the symbol for gold is Au, which comes from an abbreviation of *aurum*, the Latin name for gold.

As you can see, there are many ways to refer to an atom that has 79 protons: gold, Au, atomic number 79, or Z = 79. Sometimes to be extra clear, the atomic number is displayed as a subscript to the *left* of the chemical symbol, as in $_1H$, $_2He$, or $_{79}Au$. This notation tells you right away what the atomic number is, so we will frequently use it in the chapters that follow. Often the subscript is just dropped, however, since it is assumed that you can look up the atomic number for any particular chemical symbol.

MASS NUMBER AND NEUTRON NUMBER

Even if two atoms have the same number of protons, they can have different numbers of neutrons. Two such atoms are called **isotopes** of a given element. The **neutron number** is given the symbol N. The total number of particles in the nucleus is given by the sum of the number of protons and the number of neutrons. This sum is called the **atomic mass number** and is represented by

What's in a Name (or Symbol)?

The chemical symbols for many common elements closely resemble their English names. For example, beryllium is Be, nitrogen is N, and oxygen is O. There are other common elements, however, whose symbols don't closely match their English names. We already mentioned that gold has the symbol Au from its Latin name *aurum*. Other elements with symbols that more closely resemble their Latin names are silver (Ag, from *argentum*), copper (Cu, from *cuprum*), potassium (K, from *kalium*), sodium (Na, from *natrium*), iron (Fe, from *ferrum*), and tin (Sn, from *stannum*). Some elements are named for the places in which they were discovered. Gallium (Ga) was named for *Gallia*, the Latin name for France. Similarly, germanium (Ge) and scandium (Sc) were named after Germany and Scandinavia. Polonium (Po) was named after Poland, the birthplace of its discoverer, Marie Curie. Some more recently discovered elements are named californium (Cf) and berkelium (Bk) after Berkeley, California, home of the University of California, Berkeley, where many elements with high atomic numbers have been artificially produced. Finally, some elements have been named to honor famous scientists: einsteinium (Es) for Albert Einstein, fermium (Fm) for Enrico Fermi, curium (Cm) for Marie and Pierre Curie, mendelevium (Md) for Dmitry Mendeleyev, and meitnerium (Mt) for Lise Meitner, to mention only some of them.

the symbol A. For example, the most common form of carbon is carbon-12. The 12 refers to the mass number. Since carbon has atomic number 6, it has 6 protons. Carbon-12 must have 6 neutrons as well, because the number of neutrons plus the number of protons equals the mass number, 12. The mass number of an atom is often shown as a superscript to the left of the chemical symbol. Thus carbon-12 would be written as $^{12}_{6}C$. You may have heard about carbon-14 dating. Carbon-14, or $^{14}_{6}C$, is an isotope of carbon. Since it is still carbon, it must have 6 protons as indicated by the lower number. But since A = 14 we see that $^{14}_{6}C$ must have 14 − 6 = 8 neutrons, two more than ^{12}C. These examples demonstrate the general equation

$$A = Z + N$$

which means "the mass number is equal to the sum of the atomic number and the neutron number."

Nuclear masses are measured in **atomic mass units,** which are represented by the symbol u. The size of an atomic mass unit is defined so that the mass of a $^{12}_{6}C$ atom is *exactly* 12 u. Since $^{12}_{6}C$ has 6 protons and 6 neutrons, and the protons and neutrons are responsible for most of the mass of the atom, that means that protons and neutrons each weigh just about 1 u each, though not exactly. The mass of a proton is m_p = 1.0073 u and the mass of a neutron is m_n = 1.0087 u. The mass of $^{13}_{6}C$ is 13.0034 u, while the mass of $^{238}_{92}U$ is 238.0508 u. Thus, the atomic mass number does give the approximate mass of the atom or nucleus in atomic mass units, u. If you want you can convert that into a more familiar unit of mass, the kilogram: 1 u = 1.66 × 10^{-27} kg.

IONS

Finally, two atoms that are the same element and the same isotope might still have different numbers of electrons. This will affect the net charge of the atom. Neutral atoms have equal numbers of electrons and protons. If the number of electrons is different from the number of protons, the atom is said to be ionized. The number of electrons isn't given its own symbol. Instead the net charge— namely, the number of protons minus the number of electrons—is written as a superscript to the right of the chemical symbol, as in Li^+. Here's an everyday example. Consider the salt in the salt shaker sitting on the kitchen table. The scientific name for salt is sodium chloride. The name comes from the atoms that make up salt, namely sodium ($_{11}Na$) and chlorine ($_{17}Cl$). Usually the sodium and chlorine atoms are stuck tightly together in a crystal. But when

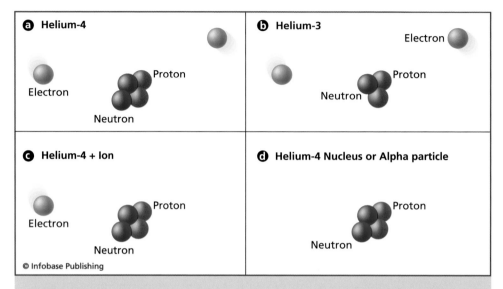

Figure 3.1 *Isotopes and ions of helium. (a) The most common helium atom, $_2^4$He. It has a mass number of four because in addition to two protons, the nucleus contains two neutrons. (b) An isotope of helium with one fewer neutron in the nucleus, $_2^3$He. (c) A single ionized helium-4 ion, $_2^4$He$^+$ is positively charged because it has two protons but only one electron. (d) In a double ionized helium-4 ion, $_2^4$He^{++}, both electrons are missing, so it has a positive charge of +2.*

you dissolve salt into a glass of water, the sodium and chlorine atoms separate into sodium ions, Na$^+$, and chlorine ions, Cl$^-$. Sodium has atomic number 11, so the Na$^+$ ion has 11 protons. Since it is positively charged it must have 10 electrons altogether. On the other hand, the chlorine ion is negatively charged, which means it has one *extra* electron. Since chlorine has 17 protons (atomic number 17) that means Cl$^-$ must have 18 electrons. There can also be ions with greater electric charge, like He^{++}, which is the nucleus of a helium atom (Z = 2) where *both* the electrons have been removed. An atom that has had one electron removed is said to be **ionized**, and He^{++} is doubly ionized. Such a helium nucleus is also known as an alpha particle. (Recall that Rutherford used alpha particles in his discovery of the nucleus, described previously.)

In summary, atoms are usually described by specifying their chemical symbol, atomic number, mass number, and net charge. Thus, a generic atom of type X would be written $^A_Z X^+$. This means that this atom of element X has Z protons, mass number A, and a net charge of +1. From this, we can determine that it also has A − Z neutrons and Z − 1 electrons. To illustrate, we will look at some isotopes and ions of helium. Figure 3.1a shows the most common form of helium, $^4_2$He. Figure 3.1b shows a lighter isotope of helium that has one less neutron, $^3_2$He. Figure 3.1c shows the $^4_2$He$^+$ ion, which has one less electron than the usual helium atom. Last, Figure 3.1d shows the helium nucleus or alpha particle, $^4_2$He^{++}.

CHAPTER 4

The Periodic Table of the Elements

IN 1869, A YOUNG MAN FROM SIBERIA WITH A LONG BEARD and wild hair brought order to the chaos of nineteenth-century chemistry. Dmitry Mendeleyev was born in 1834 into a large family in Tobolsk, Siberia (Figure 4.1). When he was still young, his family came on hard times. After his father died, he and his mother hitchhiked 4,000 miles (6,437 km) to St. Petersburg so he could attend school. After diligent work at his studies and as a teacher, he eventually joined the university, where he was perhaps as much known for his unkempt appearance as for his work on chemistry. But in 1869, at the age of 35, Mendeleyev's work during the previous decade paid off when he struck upon a wonderful scheme for organizing the bewildering array of elements that chemists studied. He collected all 63 of the elements known at the time into a neat, rectangular grid. The elements were organized in order of increasing atomic mass in one direction and grouped by chemical properties in the other direction. The order embodied in the periodic table was pleasing but also surprising. It was as if half of the pieces in a 100-piece jigsaw puzzle suddenly snapped into place. Nobody knew why the atoms should fit into such a neat grid.

Figure 4.1 *Dmitry Mendeleyev was a Russian chemist credited as the creator of the first version of the periodic table of the elements.*

Before Mendeleyev, chemists already knew that there were some materials that were more fundamental than others. Some things, like salt, could be easily separated into other materials, in this case, sodium and chlorine. But try as they might, chemists couldn't break the sodium or chlorine into anything else. As discussed in Chapter 2, such indivisible substances are called elements. Thanks to John Dalton, it was generally accepted that each elemental substance was made up of many individual atoms, all with characteristics unique to that element. At that time, however, nobody really knew what an atom was. All they knew was that each element had different properties, like its color or whether it was solid, liquid, or gas at room temperature. Chemists also knew that the atoms from different elements all had different masses. This seemingly random collection of atoms with different masses and different properties was utterly confusing. Mendeleyev ordered the elements by mass while grouping similar elements together. This arrangement revealed a hidden pattern: As Mendeleyev looked at the list of atoms by increasing mass, he saw that most atoms shared many properties with the atoms eight places behind them and eight places ahead of them. In fact, the periodic table worked so well that Mendeleyev could boldly predict the mass and properties of three new elements that had never been observed but were needed to fill some holes in his table. A few years later, the discoveries of the elements gallium, germanium, and scandium brilliantly vindicated Mendeleyev's predictions.

To date, more than 100 elements have been observed, nearly twice as many as Mendeleyev knew about. But the amazing thing is that all of the more recent discoveries can be added to the periodic table of elements following Mendeleyev's scheme. This yields the modern version shown in Figure 4.2. His method of organizing the elements is both powerful and useful because the position of an element in the periodic table gives an indication of its properties, allowing scientists to predict how it will react when combined with other elements. This chapter will explain the principles behind the periodic table in terms of modern atomic theory, something that was not available to Mendeleyev back in 1869.

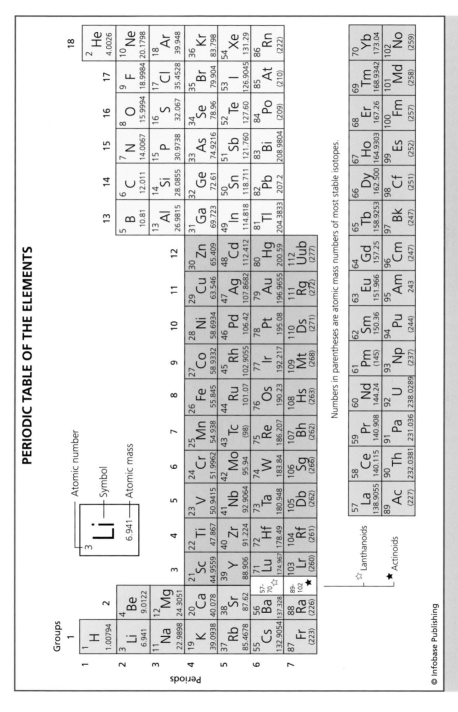

Figure 4.2 *The modern periodic table is a tabular method of displaying the chemical elements.*

Physics Through History: Who Gets the Credit?

Mendeleyev is usually given the credit for discovering the periodic table of the elements, and it is true that his contributions were of critical importance. Many other people, however, were also seeking to find order in the confusing list of different atoms. Shortly before Mendeleyev published his table, the Englishman John Newlands had noticed the repetition in the properties of the elements when listed by atomic mass. But his observations were ridiculed because he likened the repetition of elemental properties to the repetition of octaves on a piano keyboard. A German scientist, Lothar Meyer, independently devised a periodic table that was very similar to Mendeleyev's and published just a year later. This is a good example of how difficult it can be to determine who deserves the credit for making a scientific discovery. Newlands had clearly hit upon the fundamental order hiding within the elements, but was unable to convince anyone of the usefulness of his observation. Meyer also successfully organized the elements into a table using his own insight and understanding. But it is Mendeleyev who brought the orderliness of the elements to the attention of the chemists worldwide, particularly through his bold predictions for new elements that were yet to be discovered. These are some of the reasons why Mendeleyev usually gets the credit for discovering the periodic table.

QUANTUM NUMBERS

The periodic table organizes atoms based on their mass and their chemical properties. The mass is determined by the size of the nucleus, which is related to the atomic number. The chemical properties are determined by the electrons. Every neutral atom has the same number of electrons as it has protons. But those electrons cannot be located just anywhere outside the nucleus. They can only occupy very precisely determined regions depending on their energy. The existence of these allowed orbits was predicted by Bohr's model of the atom and later understood more precisely using the machinery of quantum mechanics. The restriction of electrons to specific energy levels is responsible for the peculiar structure of the periodic table.

The allowed electron energy levels are labeled by four **quantum numbers** that give the address of an electron in an atom. The first is the principal quantum number, n, which we met before in the discussion of the Bohr model. The principal quantum number can be any integer starting with one, $n = 1, 2, 3. \ldots$. The larger the principal quantum number, the higher the energy of the electron and the farther it is from the nucleus. Each value of n corresponds to an energy shell that can hold more than one electron. The space within each shell is divided into **subshells** that are labeled by the second number, called the **angular momentum quantum number**, denoted l. For each shell specified by n, the value of l can be any integer between 0 and $n - 1$. For example, in the $n = 3$ shell, there are subshells with $l = 0, 1$, and 2. Confusingly, for historical reasons, the subshells are often labeled by a letter instead of a number. In this alternative notation, s, p, d, and f refer to $l = 0, 1, 2$, and 3, respectively. That means the $n = 3$ shell mentioned before contains s, p, and d subshells. Finally, each subshell is further divided up based on the **magnetic quantum number**, m_l, which is allowed to be an integer between $-l$ and l. Together these first three quantum numbers, n, l, and m_l specify an orbital, the physical location of an electron within an atom. The fourth quantum number, m_s, can be either $+1/2$ or $-1/2$. It refers to a peculiar property of electrons called **spin**. Each orbital can hold up to two electrons as long as they don't both have the same value of m_s. (See the "Spinning Electrons?" sidebar for more details about spin.)

The values of n, l, m_l, and m_s for a particular electron specify exactly which energy level it is in. Continuing with the above example, for the shell with $n = 3$, there is one orbital with $l = 0$ and $m_l = 0$, called the "3s" orbital, which can hold two electrons, one with $m_s = +1/2$ and the other with $m_s = -1/2$. There are also three orbitals corresponding to $l = 1$ and $m_l = -1$, 0, or 1, called the "3p" orbitals. Finally, there are five orbitals corresponding to $l = 2$ and $m_l = -2, -1$, 0, 1, or 2 which are called the "3d" orbitals. In each of these orbitals an electron can have either $m_s = +1/2$ or $m_s = -1/2$. The complicated pattern of allowed quantum numbers is summarized in Table 4.1, which shows all the orbitals corresponding to $n \leq 4$.

TABLE 4.1		Allowed Quantum Numbers and the Number of Electrons That Can Occupy Each Subshell			
n	l	m_l	m_s	SUBSHELL NAME	NUMBER OF ELECTRONS
1	0	0	+1/2, -1/2	1s	2
2	0	0	+1/2, -1/2	2s	2
2	1	-1, 0, 1	+1/2, -1/2	2p	6
3	0	0	+1/2, -1/2	3s	2
3	1	-1, 0, 1	+1/2, -1/2	3p	6
3	2	-2, -1, 0, 1, 2	+1/2, -1/2	3d	10
4	0	0	+1/2, -1/2	4s	2
4	1	-1, 0, 1	+1/2, -1/2	4p	6
4	2	-2, -1, 0, 1, 2	+1/2, -1/2	4d	10
4	3	-3, -2, -1, 0, 1, 2, 3	+1/2, -1/2	4f	14

BUILDING AN ATOM

Imagine that we wanted to build an atom out of its components. We would start with a certain number of protons, thereby determining which element it is. Then we would add some neutrons to form the nucleus. Finally, we would need to add some electrons. Though the structure of the electron energy levels is rather complicated, the electrons follow a simple rule to decide which orbitals they should occupy. The rule is: Minimize energy. So if you add an electron to an atom, it will occupy the lowest energy orbital that is allowed by the **exclusion principle** (see sidebar on page 42). The energy of an orbital is determined by n and l. Larger values of n mean higher energy, so the 3s subshell has higher energy than the 2s, which in turn has higher energy than the 1s subshell. Also, for a given value of n, the higher l values have higher energy. Thus, the s subshell has the lowest energy, while the p, d, and f subshells have increasing energy. The magnetic and spin quantum numbers, m_l and m_s, do not affect the energy, but they determine how many electrons are allowed in a given subshell.

To make a neutral atom, we would need a number of electrons equal to the atomic number. Then we would just start dropping the electrons in, and they would fill up the lowest energy levels available. The first two electrons would fill up the 1s subshell, as shown in the first row of Table 4.1. The next two would go into the 2s subshell. The next six electrons could all fit into the 2p subshell. We would just continue filling up orbitals until we ran out of electrons.

This procedure gets a little more complicated when we get to atoms with more than 18 electrons. The first 18 electrons fill up the 1s, 2s, 2p, 3s, and 3p subshells. However, the next two electrons go into the 4s subshell instead of the 3d subshell, as you might expect by looking at Table 4.1. The reason is that the 4s subshell actually has lower energy than the 3d subshell. But after the 4s subshell is full, the next 10 electrons all go into the 3d subshell. The order in which the subshells are filled is shown in Table 4.2.

Spinning Electrons?

*E*lectrons are elementary particles with a very small mass that carry a negative electrical charge. They also have another property called spin, which can have one of two values, +1/2 or −1/2, sometimes also called spin up and spin down. The name spin is a bit deceptive, because the electron isn't really rotating. Instead, it is as if the electron had a tiny bar magnet inside of it. If there is a magnetic field nearby, the electron's internal magnet can either point in the same direction as the magnetic field (spin up or m_s = +1/2) or in the opposite direction (spin down or m_s = −1/2). You might think that the internal magnet could make a different angle with the magnetic field, but because of quantum mechanics, spin up and spin down are the only two possibilities. For this reason it is better to just think of spin as a new quantum mechanical property of the electron that can take one of two values.

This new property has interesting consequences. It turns out that because of their spin, electrons don't like to be packed too closely together. This "antisocial" behavior of electrons is a result of the exclusion principle, which was suggested in 1925 by Wolfgang Pauli and eventually earned him the 1945 Nobel Prize in Physics. The exclusion principle states that no two electrons can have all the same quantum numbers. For example, any electron in the n = 1 shell must have l = 0 and m_l = 0. Thus, if one electron in that 1s orbital has m_s = +1/2, there is only enough room left for one more electron, and that electron *must* have m_s = −1/2.

Look again at the periodic table in Figure 4.2. The rows in the periodic table are called **periods**. The periodic table starts in the upper left hand corner with hydrogen, the element with atomic number Z = 1. The atomic number of the elements increases from left to right and from top to bottom. Since the number of electrons in a neutral atom is equal to the atomic number, this means that the number of electrons also increases in the

TABLE 4.2 Subshells of the Rows of the Periodic Table

ROW (PERIOD)	SUBSHELLS*	NUMBER OF ELEMENTS
1	1s	2
2	2s, 2p	2+6=8
3	3s, 3p	2+6=8
4	4s, 3d, 4p	2+10+6=18
5	5s, 4d, 5p	2+10+6=18
6	6s, 4f, 5d, 6p	2+14+10+6=32
7	7s, 5f, 6d, 7p	2+14+10+6=32

*The subshells are shown with increasing energy, from top to bottom and left to right.

same way. The unusual shape of the periodic table is dictated by the electronic structure.

The easiest way to see how all this works is by looking at some simple examples, starting with hydrogen. The single electron in hydrogen occupies the lowest energy orbital in the 1s subshell. The next element, helium, has two electrons, and both of them can fit in the 1s subshell. Hydrogen and helium are the two elements in the first row of the periodic table, period 1. They correspond to atoms whose last electrons are placed in the 1s subshell. The next element, lithium, has three electrons. Two electrons go into the 1s subshell, but then that subshell is full, so the third electron has to go into the 2s subshell. Lithium is the first atom to have any electrons in the $n = 2$ shell, so it is placed at the beginning of the second row, period 2. The next element is beryllium, which has four electrons. Two of them fill up the 1s subshell, and

Physics Lab: Edible Elements?

*B*reakfast cereal is often fortified with vitamins and minerals that are important for a healthy diet. Some of the nutrients are complicated molecules formed out of many different types of atoms. Other nutrients are atoms of a specific element. Take a look at the "Nutrition Facts" label on your breakfast cereal or some other food. How many of the nutrients listed there can you find in the periodic table of the elements? One example is iron, $_{26}$Fe, which is located in the middle of the fourth row of the periodic table. Iron is important for making red blood cells. On the other hand, you won't be able to find vitamin C in the periodic table. Vitamin C is a complicated molecule made up of carbon, hydrogen, and oxygen atoms that is important for building bones, teeth, and muscles.

the next two fill up the 2s subshell. The next six elements have more electrons than beryllium, so they start putting their additional electrons into the 2p subshell. Neon is the last element in period 2. It has 10 electrons that fill the 1s, 2s, and 2p subshells. Because the next element, sodium, has one more electron than neon, it must put this last electron into the 3s subshell. Since sodium is the first atom to have any electrons in the $n = 3$ shell, it is placed at the beginning of a new period, period 3.

This process continues for all of the elements in the periodic table. For every neutral atom there are as many electrons as protons, and those electrons fill up the allowed orbitals starting with the lowest energy orbitals first. The order that the orbitals are filled is shown in Table 4.2, which also shows the correspondence to the periods in the periodic table. The first row, period 1, corresponds to the two elements that have electrons only in the 1s subshell. Period 2 has eight elements, those that put their last electrons in the 2s or 2p subshells. Period 3 also has eight elements corresponding to the filling of the 3s and 3p subshells.

Period 4 gets complicated. It has 18 elements, corresponding to the filling of the 4s, 3d, and 4p subshells. Period 5 is similar to period 4, since the 5s, 4d, and 5p subshells are filled. Something new happens in period 6. Period 6 contains elements that have filled all of the electron orbitals up to 5p and start to fill the 6s, 4f, 5d, and 6p subshells. The 14 elements corresponding to the filling of the 4f subshell, however, are often set off from the rest of the table. They are rare elements that all have similar properties. The same thing happens in period 7. After the 7s subshell is full, the 14 elements that start to fill the 5f subshell are also set off from the rest of the table. The other thing about period 7 is that it is only partly filled because some of the elements needed to complete the row have never been observed.

By always filling up the lowest energy levels while never allowing two electrons to have the same values of n, l, m_l, and m_s we can build up the electron configuration for any element in the periodic table. The inherent order in these electron configurations underlies Mendeleyev's magnificent organization of the elements in the periodic table. In the next chapter, we will see how the location of an element in the periodic table gives information about its chemical properties.

CHAPTER 5

Chemical Bonds

LET'S THINK SOME MORE ABOUT TABLE SALT, ALSO KNOWN as sodium chloride, or NaCl. A certain amount of salt is essential for your body to function properly. Too much salt can be bad, but so can too little. One interesting thing about table salt is that it is made up of some rather dangerous chemicals. If you could separate salt into its constituent elements, you would be left with chlorine gas, which is poisonous to breathe, and metallic sodium, which is highly **reactive**. In the case of sodium, reactive means that when it comes in contact with water it fizzes and sparks, and if there is enough sodium, it can explode and catch fire. Since your body has lots of water in it, it's a good thing that the sodium in your body doesn't behave in that way! Why is it that some elements like sodium form solids that explode when they come in contact with water, while other elements like chlorine form a gas that is poisonous? How can these two dangerous elements come together to form something like table salt that helps the human body function and makes food taste better? In this section we will explore how to predict the ways in which elements react and which ones will fit together.

CHEMICAL FORMULAE

How do the different atoms make up the millions of different substances that we see around us every day? They do this by combining in many different ways to form various molecules and compounds. An example of one such compound is table salt, sodium chloride. The two types of atoms in sodium chloride are sodium, $_{11}$Na, and chlorine, $_{17}$Cl, which are stuck together in a regular pattern, as shown in Figure 5.1. This pattern is repeated over and

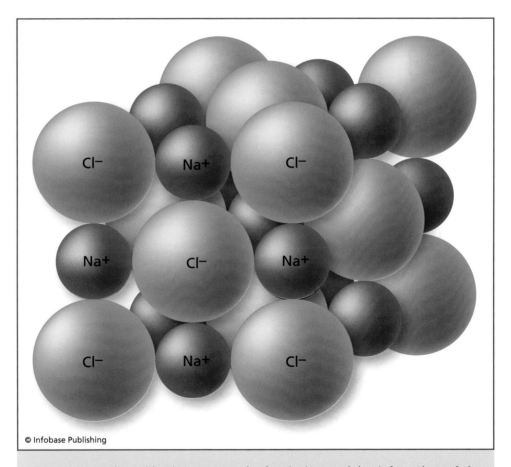

© Infobase Publishing

Figure 5.1 *Sodium chloride is an example of an ionic crystal that is formed out of alternating positively and negatively charged ions.*

over within the salt crystals you put on your food. This kind of compound is specified by simply listing the constituent atoms. So the **chemical formula** for sodium chloride is indicated by NaCl.

Other compounds are formed of basic units called molecules. Molecules are formed by different elements bonding together to form a larger structure. The resulting molecules can have very different properties from the individual atoms that make them up. We got a glance at water molecules in Figure 1.1. The chemical formula for a molecule consists of the chemical symbols of the constituent atoms with a subscript to the *right* of each symbol to indicate how many atoms of that type appear in the molecule. Since a water molecule is made up of two atoms of hydrogen and one atom of oxygen, its chemical formula is H_2O. Carbon dioxide has one atom of carbon and two atoms of oxygen, so it is written CO_2. When writing the chemical formula for a molecule, the atomic number and mass number are not included with the chemical symbol; otherwise, it would be too confusing. A more complicated molecule is $C_6H_{12}O_6$, which represents fructose, the sugar found in fruits. Each molecule of fructose has 6 carbon atoms, 12 hydrogen atoms, and 6 oxygen atoms, all stuck together in a specific way by chemical bonds. In order to understand molecules, we need to understand the bonds between their atoms. And to understand bonds we need to look closely at the electron energy levels.

FILLED AND EMPTY SHELLS

We saw in Chapter 4 that the structure of the periodic table is linked to the electronic structure of the elements. Each atom has its electrons arranged in consecutive energy levels that get further and further from the nucleus. The lowest shells are filled with electrons first, but as they become full, the higher shells are filled. The highest shell that contains any electrons is called the **valence shell**, and the electrons occupying the valence shell are called the **valence electrons**. It is the valence electrons that determine the chemical properties of an atom. All the other electrons in the atom that occupy the lower, filled shells, have very little effect on the atom's properties.

As an example, consider the element calcium ($_{20}Ca$). It is the second element in the fourth row, or period. Because it has atomic number 20, a neutral calcium atom must have 20 electrons surrounding its nucleus. Two of those 20 electrons fill up the lowest, $n = 1$ shell, which you can think of as being represented by the first row of the periodic table. The next eight electrons fill up the $n = 2$ shell, corresponding to the second period. The third period also has eight spaces, corresponding to the eight electrons needed to fill the third shell. So far we've accounted for $2 + 8 + 8 = 18$ of the electrons in calcium, leaving only two more that we have to account for. They start filling up the fourth shell, which means that calcium has two valence electrons and they inhabit the fourth shell.

The rows or periods in the periodic table correspond to the consecutive electron shells that get filled up as you move to the right. That means that the column or *group* corresponds to the number of electrons in the valence shell. The modern way of labeling the groups is by the Arabic numerals 1 through 18, with group 1 being the left hand column and group 18 being the far right hand column. Notice that the first three rows don't have elements in all of the groups. This is due to the restrictions on the values of the quantum number l.

Since the number of valence electrons determines an atom's chemical properties, and all of the atoms in each group (column) have the same number of valence electrons, they should all have similar properties. In particular, how reactive an element is depends on how full its valence shell is. The guiding principle is that atoms want to have full valence shells. Atoms with almost full valence shells really want to fill them up, and they do this by trying to steal electrons from other nearby atoms. On the other hand, atoms with just one or two electrons in the outer shell are glad to get rid of their excess electrons. After giving away excess electrons, they are left with a full shell that is closer to the nucleus. This tendency to either give up or acquire more electrons is what leads to the very different properties exhibited by different elements.

Extra Electrons

Let's look at group 1, the left-most column of the periodic table. It contains hydrogen ($_1$H), lithium ($_3$Li), sodium ($_{11}$Na), potassium ($_{19}$K), rubidium ($_{37}$Rb), cesium ($_{55}$Cs), and francium ($_{87}$Fr). These elements are called **alkali metals,** and they each have exactly one valence electron. Since the atoms would prefer to have a full outer shell, they could either acquire many extra electrons to fill up the valence shell, or they could get rid of the one extra electron. It turns out to be much easier to donate that one extra electron than to collect more, so that's what usually happens. This eagerness to donate an electron is what make these elements in the first column of the periodic table very reactive. In other words, they easily combine with other atoms to make compounds. Notice that sodium, the explosive component of table salt, sits in the first column.

Moving over to the second column in the periodic table, we encounter the **alkaline earth metals**, elements that all have 2 valence electrons. These elements include beryllium ($_4$Be), magnesium ($_{12}$Mg), calcium ($_{20}$Ca), strontium ($_{38}$Sr), barium ($_{56}$Ba), and radium ($_{88}$Ra). These atoms would also prefer to give up their two extra electrons to get down to a full outer shell with lower energy. This makes them also quite reactive.

Vacancies

In any given row of the periodic table, each step to the right adds another electron to the atom, gradually filling up the valence shell. In Group 17, the second to last column, we find the elements fluorine ($_9$F), chlorine ($_{17}$Cl), bromine ($_{35}$Br), iodine ($_{53}$I), and astatine ($_{85}$At). They are called the **halogens**, and each of them has a valence shell that is only one electron shy of being full. The halogens would really like to acquire an electron from another atom to fill up their valence shell, and this makes them highly reactive. That is what makes chlorine gas dangerous. When you inhale it, the chlorine atoms start to break up molecules in your nose, throat, and lungs in order to gain extra electrons.

The Noble Gases

Finally, we reach the last column, Group 18. We saw above that helium ($_2$He) has 2 electrons, completely filling the $n = 1$ shell. Therefore helium is quite satisfied as it is and doesn't try to either give up or acquire more electrons. This makes it quite unreactive.

Beyond Balloons: The Importance of Helium

Helium is a noble gas, which means it is found in the far right column of the periodic table. Because helium has a full valence shell, it is inert, which means it is very unreactive. But that doesn't mean it isn't useful. Most people are familiar with helium because it is used to fill balloons to make them float. If inhaled, it also will make your voice high and squeaky. But helium also has more practical applications. Because it is so unreactive, it can be useful for creating a very clean atmosphere for producing microelectronics. Helium also has the lowest boiling point of any element, just 4.2 degrees above absolute zero (that's -269°C or -452°F!), which means it is an important low-temperature coolant. It is especially important for cooling materials to allow them to become superconducting and thereby produce large magnetic fields. Those magnetic fields are important for medical imaging techniques. Helium is produced by radioactive decay happening inside the Earth. The helium gas that is given off collects in caverns along with natural gas, so it is collected by companies that drill natural gas wells. Unfortunately, there isn't an unending supply of helium on the Earth. Because helium is so light, once it percolates out of the ground, it floats around in the atmosphere and eventually escapes into space. Because of the importance of helium, the U.S. government maintains a permanent reserve of 17 million cubic meters of helium.

The same is true of neon ($_{10}$Ne), argon ($_{18}$Ar), krypton ($_{36}$Kr), xenon ($_{54}$Xe), and radon ($_{86}$Rn). Because they are so stable, these elements were named the inert or **noble gases**.

Sharing Electrons

The elements in the middle columns of the periodic table, groups 3 to 16, are generally not as reactive as the alkali metals or the halogens. These middle elements have partially filled valence shells and could either gain or lose electrons. In reality, these elements tend to share electrons with other atoms in order to reach a full valence shell. In this way, some electrons do double duty, filling up the valence shell for several atoms. The shared electrons are essentially part of both atoms.

From these examples, we can see that there is a range of possibilities for how atoms treat their valence electrons. Some elements happily give up their valence electrons completely, while others share them equally with another atom, and still other elements seek to gain valence electrons from nearby atoms. Roughly speaking, the elements on the left side of the periodic table are more willing to give up their valence electrons while those elements on the right side would rather acquire more electrons. Even when atoms are sharing electrons, some atoms will tend to attract the electrons closer to their nucleus. **Electronegativity** is the measure of how strongly an atom pulls shared electrons towards itself. Thus elements in the first column like sodium have smaller electronegativities than the atoms in the second to last column, like chlorine. Elements in the middle of the table like silver, aluminum, or carbon have intermediate values of electronegativity.

TYPES OF BONDS

Ionic Bonds

Remember sodium chloride (table salt), which we discussed at the beginning of the chapter? It is made up of sodium, an element in the first column of the periodic table that has one extra electron, and chlorine, an element in the second to last column

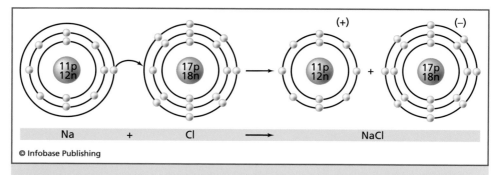

Na   +   Cl   ⟶   NaCl

© Infobase Publishing

Figure 5.2 *An ionic bond is formed when an electron from a sodium atom is transferred to an atom of chlorine. The resulting positive sodium ion and negative chlorine ion are attracted to each other to form an ionic bond.*

that is only one electron shy of having a full valence shell. As we discussed, both of these elements by themselves are highly reactive and dangerous, but together they form the stable, unreactive compound that we use in our kitchen and dining rooms. This is because sodium and chlorine are made for each other. The sodium atom gives its extra electron to a chlorine atom, leaving two atoms with filled valence shells. This is why the salt on your table is not nearly so exciting (or dangerous) as either sodium or chlorine alone. But because each atom now has a different number of electrons than protons, they are both charged ions. Since sodium loses an electron. we are left with a positively charged sodium ion, Na^+. Similarly, the chlorine atom has one excess electron, giving it a net negative charge, Cl^-. Once this happens, the electric force that causes opposite charges to attract each other pulls the positive sodium ion and the negative chlorine ion together to form what is called an **ionic bond**. This is shown schematically in Figure 5.2.

In general, ionic bonds form when extra electrons leave one type of atom to join with another type of atom. The resulting atoms are both ionized, which means they have excess electrical charge. The atom that gives up the electron is positively charged and the atom that accepts the electron is negatively charged. They are then attracted to each other by the electrostatic force.

Ionic solids are formed out of a regular pattern of ions like the salt crystal shown in Figure 5.1. Each atom in the crystal has an ionic bond between itself and each of its neighbors. It requires a lot of energy to remove any single atom from the crystal, making it quite strong. However, such crystals readily separate into their respective ions when they are dissolved in water. If you take the NaCl crystals in your salt shaker and put them in water, the water is able to break the salt crystals apart into Na^+ and Cl^- ions.

Covalent Bonds

Some atoms that do not want to give up their outer electrons are still willing to share one or more electrons with another atom. Bonds that result when outer shell electrons are shared between two atoms are called **covalent bonds**. Covalent bonds are generally quite strong.

For example, consider the water molecules that we zoomed in on earlier. Each molecule was composed of hydrogen and oxygen. A hydrogen atom has one electron, but would really like to get one more to have a full $n = 1$, $l = 0$ valence shell with two electrons in it. On the other hand, oxygen has six electrons in its valence shell, two in the 2s ($n = 2$, $l = 0$) subshell and four in the 2p ($n = 2$, $l = 1$) subshell. The 2s subshell is full, but the 2p subshell can hold six electrons. Since the oxygen atom only has four electrons in its 2p subshell, it still needs two electrons to fill its valence shell. To make the hydrogen and oxygen atoms happy, each oxygen atom finds two atoms of hydrogen to bond with. The oxygen atom borrows one electron from each of the hydrogen atoms, filling its outer shell. Simultaneously, the hydrogen atoms each borrow an electron from the oxygen atom, giving them two electrons and a full valence shell. This is shown schematically in Figure 5.3a. Thus for each hydrogen atom there is a pair of electrons that is shared with the oxygen atom, one electron in the pair contributed by the hydrogen and one contributed by the oxygen. Because the two atoms are sharing the same two electrons, they can't move too

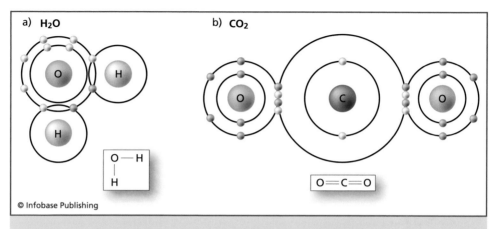

Figure 5.3 *(a) A water molecule is held together by covalent bonds between each hydrogen atom and the oxygen atom. In each bond, a pair of electrons is shared by the hydrogen and oxygen atoms. (b) A double covalent bond forms from the sharing of two pairs of electrons between each oxygen atom and the carbon atom in carbon dioxide.*

far apart and are thus stuck together. This shared pair of electrons forms a covalent bond. In the water molecule there is a covalent bond between each hydrogen atom and the oxygen atom.

Often a covalent bond will be represented symbolically as a line joining the two atoms that are sharing a pair of electrons. Thus the bond between the oxygen and hydrogen atoms is shown as: O—H. More complicated bonding arrangements can also be shown, as in Figure 5.3a for the water molecule.

Two atoms can share more than one pair of electrons, and thus form a stronger bond. A **double bond** forms when two pairs of electrons are shared between the same two atoms. This means that four electrons are being shared, with each atom contributing two electrons. For example, carbon dioxide (CO_2) is made up of one carbon atom and two oxygen atoms. Carbon has 4 electrons in its valence shell, two in the 2s ($n = 2$, $l = 0$) subshell and two in the 2p ($n = 2$, $l = 1$) subshell. Oxygen, located two columns over in the same row, has two more electrons and thus six electrons in its outer shell. Both carbon and oxygen need eight electrons in their valence shell for it to be full. Thus, carbon needs four more electrons and each oxygen needs two electrons. What happens is that each oxygen atom shares two of its electrons with the carbon atom, and the carbon atom shares two of its electrons with each of the oxygen atoms, forming a covalent double bond between the carbon and each oxygen atom. The carbon now has four of its own valence electrons, plus two shared electrons from each of the two oxygen atoms, giving it eight outer electrons and a full valence shell. Each oxygen atom has six of its own valence electrons plus two of the carbon atom's electrons that it is sharing, also giving the oxygen atom a full valence shell with eight electrons. This is shown in Figure 5.3b. A double bond between two atoms is represented as a double line connecting the chemical symbols. Thus another way of writing CO_2 is $O=C=O$.

Even more electrons can be shared, though this is much less common. A triple bond is formed when three pairs of electrons are shared between atoms, and a quadruple bond has four shared pairs. These are symbolically represented by three or four lines joining two chemical symbols. For example, a triple bond appears between the carbon atoms in an acetylene molecule, $H-C\equiv C-H$.

Polarization

As discussed in the previous section, a covalent bond arises when a pair of electrons is shared between two atoms. Those two electrons, however, need not be shared equally. Recall the concept of electronegativity from Chapter 4. Atoms that have a higher electronegativity tend to pull the electrons in a covalent bond closer to themselves. When this happens a molecule can become **polarized**, which means that the positive and negative electrical charges in the molecule are slightly separated.

Water molecules serve as an excellent example. The two hydrogen atoms in a water molecule are each stuck to the oxygen atom by a covalent bond, and the angle between those two bonds is 104.5°. The oxygen is more electronegative than the hydrogen atoms, and so the shared electrons are drawn closer to the oxygen atom. This means even though the molecule itself is neutral, there is a slight excess negative charge near the oxygen end of the molecule and an equal but opposite excess of positive charge near the two hydrogen atoms, as shown in Figure 5.4. This separation of charge, or polarization, happens naturally in a water molecule, so we say that water is a polar molecule. Polarity plays an important role in hydrogen bonds, which will be discussed in the next section.

The concepts of electronegativity and polarization are important for getting a deeper understanding of atomic bonding.

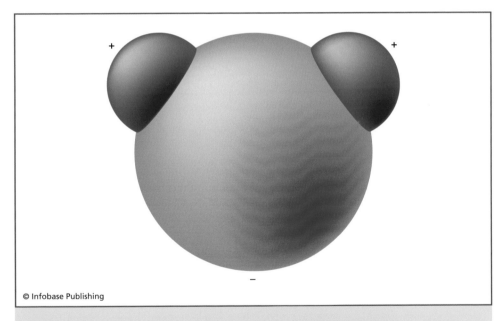

Figure 5.4 *A water molecule is a good example of a polar molecule, where there is a slight separation of positive and negative charges. In water the oxygen atom is slightly more negative because it pulls the electrons closer to itself. This leaves the hydrogen atoms slightly positive.*

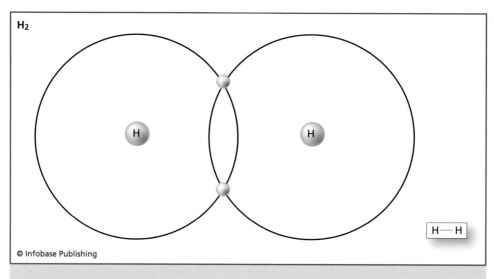

© Infobase Publishing

Figure 5.5 *The covalent bond between hydrogen atoms forms a hydrogen molecule (H₂). The pair of electrons is equally shared between the hydrogen atoms.*

So far we have talked about ionic and covalent bonds as if they are completely distinct; however, there is a continuum of bonds that fit between these extremes and make it impossible to draw a sharp line between ionic and covalent bonds. This is easiest to see with some examples. First, consider some molecules made of two identical atoms, like hydrogen gas (H_2). Each hydrogen atom has one outer electron, but it would prefer to have two electrons to have a full valence shell. Thus, two hydrogen atoms readily share their valence electrons with each other and form a covalent bond, as shown in Figure 5.5. Since the two hydrogen atoms have exactly the same electronegativity, they both attract the electrons to themselves with the same strength. This means that the two electrons really are shared equally between the two hydrogen atoms. The same thing happens with oxygen gas (O_2), except that each oxygen atom shares two electrons with the other atom, making a covalent double bond. But again, the two atoms are both oxygen, so they have the same electronegativity and thus the electrons are shared equally.

Now consider a bond between an oxygen atom and a hydrogen atom, an OH bond. We have seen before how the oxygen atom is more electronegative and pulls the shared electrons closer to itself. Thus, the hydrogen and oxygen atoms do not share the electron pair quite equally. Instead, the electrons spend more time near the oxygen. This is still called a covalent bond, but it is not purely covalent anymore because of the unequal sharing of the electrons. The unequal sharing also leads to slight polarization in the bond, with the oxygen atom being slightly negative and the hydrogen atom being slightly positive. At the other extreme is the bond between sodium and chlorine. You can think of the bond as arising from the sharing of a pair of electrons, but since the electronegativity of the chlorine atom is so much greater than that of the sodium atom, the shared electrons are effectively removed from the sodium and taken by the chlorine to make an ionic bond.

Between the extremes of perfect sharing of electron pairs in hydrogen gas (H_2) and the completely unequal sharing (ionic bond) of table salt (NaCl), there is a range of bond types where electron pairs are shared to a greater or lesser extent.

HYDROGEN BONDS

The slight polarization of bonds, as in the case of the OH bond, can lead to a more specialized type of bond called a **hydrogen bond**. This is a weak bond that results from the polarization in a molecule near hydrogen atoms. Even though the molecule is neutral, more of the negative charge is on one side of the molecule and more of the positive charge is on the opposite side. Such molecules can then be held together by electrostatic forces much like in ionic bonds, only much weaker.

Hydrogen bonds allow the molecules containing hydrogen atoms to stick to other molecules. One good example is the water molecule. It is made up of two hydrogen atoms forming covalent bonds with one oxygen atom to form a water molecule, H_2O. The more electronegative oxygen atom pulls the electrons towards itself, leaving slightly positive hydrogen atoms at the other side. This slight positive charge near the hydrogen atoms is then attracted to any negative charges around—in particular, the slightly negative side of the oxygen atom in a *different* water molecule. This is shown in Figure 5.6.

The hydrogen bonds between water molecules must be broken for the liquid to turn into gas. This bond breaking requires extra thermal energy. This is why the boiling point of water is 100°C, whereas the boiling points for the noble gases and methane (CH_4) are all below −100°C. Hydrogen bonds are also

Wacky Water

Water is an amazing substance. It covers 75% of the Earth's surface and accounts for roughly 60% of the mass of our bodies. We see water every day, in glasses for drinking, in streams and rivers, and sometimes falling from the sky as rain. It is essential for life as we know it. Water, however, is an unusual substance. When most substances freeze they get denser, but water actually becomes less dense when it freezes. This is because the water molecules in a block of ice are held together by hydrogen bonds that form between hydrogen atoms in one molecule and oxygen atoms in the neighboring molecule. Those hydrogen bonds keep the molecules in a very open structure with lots of empty space. When heat is added and the block of ice melts, the hydrogen bonds are broken, the open structure collapses, and the water molecules are able to pack together more densely. This means that when water freezes into ice it becomes less dense and floats on top of the rest of the water. This means that during winter, fish in lakes still have liquid water to swim in even when the top layers are frozen. The polar nature of water molecules also makes it a good solvent. Substances like salt or sugar readily dissolve in water.

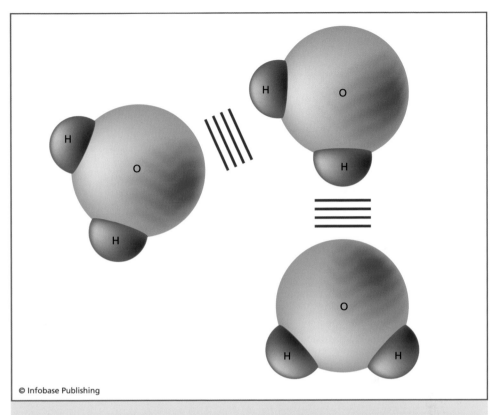

Figure 5.6 *Hydrogen bonds between water molecules form due to the attraction between the slightly positive hydrogen atoms and the slightly negative oxygen atoms.*

important for biological molecules. The genetic information of a cell is stored in DNA molecules. The DNA molecules are composed of two helical strands wrapped around each other. Hydrogen bonds form between hydrogen atoms in one strand and oxygen or nitrogen atoms in the other strand. This helps to ensure that the two strands are properly matched. This is shown in Figure 5.7.

The hydrogen bonds are critical for keeping the two strands close together and properly aligned. The DNA molecule, however,

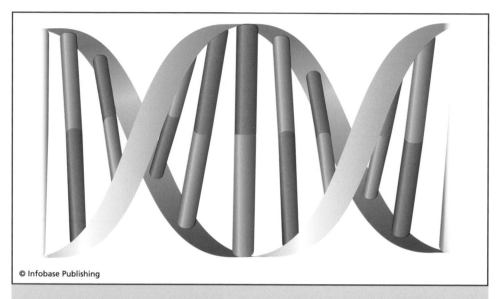

Figure 5.7 *Hydrogen bonds help hold the two strands of a DNA double helix together and keep them aligned. In this schematic drawing, the hydrogen bonds would be at the interface between blue and green regions.*

must occasionally be opened up so that the genetic code stored on each strand can be copied to make proteins. Therefore, the bonds between the two strands need to be frequently broken and cannot be too strong. Since hydrogen bonds are much weaker than the covalent bonds between the atoms within each strand, they work very well.

CHAPTER 6

Radioactivity

ALCHEMY WAS A MEDIEVAL PRACTICE THAT MIXED CHEMISTRY, philosophy, religion, and astrology with the aim of discovering a formula that would turn certain metals into gold. Begun by Greek scholars in Alexandria during the first century A.D., it spread to the Islamic world and then to Europe. By heating and distilling various materials, alchemists were trying to use chemical reactions to change one element (often lead) into another (usually gold). But we know from the previous chapters of this book that the forming and breaking of chemical bonds only involves the electrons in atoms. To change an atom from one type of element to another would require changing the number of protons in the nucleus.

It wasn't until the late 1800s that scientists got the first hints about how one element could turn into another. (Recall that they didn't even have the concept of an atomic nucleus until 1911, when Ernest Rutherford suggested the idea.) These hints came in the form of mysterious rays that were found to be emitted from certain elements. We now understand that these rays are the emission of particles and energy from an atomic nucleus when it undergoes radioactive decay.

DISCOVERY

Henri Becquerel (1852–1908) discovered that uranium salts gave off radiation that was able to expose photographic plates even when those plates were completely wrapped to keep out light. This meant that something in the uranium had penetrated the light-proof cover and left an image on the photographic film. Further experiments on uranium and similar materials revealed several types of mysterious "rays" that were emitted. At first, scientists had no idea what these rays were, so they gave them general names based on how far the ray was able to travel before it was stopped. **Alpha rays** were those that could be stopped easily, even by a piece of paper. **Beta rays** could make it through a piece of paper but were stopped by a thin sheet of metal. **Gamma rays** could penetrate the farthest and were only stopped by a thick slab of lead. Further research eventually revealed that these rays were actually streams of different types of particles, which we will discuss in more detail.

Much of the detective work into the new phenomenon of radioactivity was conducted by the physicist Marie Curie, along with her husband, Pierre, and many others. In this chapter, we will discuss the modern understanding of radioactivity and some of its practical applications and dangers.

NUCLEAR PHYSICS

The phenomena discussed so far in this book, including the periodic table and chemical bonding, are all the results of the electromagnetic forces and the activities of electrons. Radioactivity was initially mysterious in part because it is caused by the strong and weak nuclear forces at work in the nucleus of atoms. In fact, the study of radioactivity yielded lots of information about these nuclear forces and the structure of the nucleus itself.

Marie Sklodowska Curie

Born in Poland, Marie Sklo-dowska (1867–1934) moved to Paris to get a degree in physics and mathematics, and there met her husband and scientific collaborator, Pierre Curie. Marie was fascinated by the radioactivity discovered by Becquerel and sought to understand it in detail. In the process of isolating the source of the radioactivity, she discovered the element polonium, $_{84}Po$, which she named after her homeland of Poland. That discovery was announced in July 1898, and just six months later she announced the discovery of another new element, radium, $_{88}Ra$. The Curies and Becquerel were awarded the 1903 Nobel Prize in Physics for the dis-

Figure 6.1 *Marie Curie was a physicist and chemist and a pioneer in the investigation of radioactivity. She became the only person with Nobel Prizes in two different fields of science: physics and chemistry.*

covery and study of radioactivity. Marie continued to study these new elements, and by 1910 was finally able to isolate radium. In 1911, she became the first person to win two Nobel Prizes when she was awarded the Nobel Prize in Chemistry for her discovery and study of the new elements polonium and radium. The study of radioactive materials was not without its dangers, however. Pierre Curie was already experiencing symptoms of radiation sickness when he was killed in a traffic accident in 1906. Marie died of leukemia in 1934, most likely the result of all her exposure to radioactivity. Her lab notebooks absorbed so much radiation that even today they require special precautions in order to be handled safely.

Radioactivity is usually associated with elements with high atomic numbers, like radium (Ra) with atomic number Z = 88. The atomic number gives the number of protons in the nucleus, but there are also many neutrons in each nucleus. In fact, there are often more neutrons than protons, especially for the elements with large atomic numbers. The number of neutrons in a nucleus does not change the type of atom, but it does affect the stability of the nucleus. If there are too many or too few neutrons in a nucleus the atom is unstable and will undergo radioactive decay. The rate of radioactive decay is given by the **half-life** of the isotope, the time it takes for half of the atoms in a sample to decay. The decay of any one radioactive nucleus is random, but governed by the specific half-life of the material. That means that we can't know exactly when any one nucleus will decay, but on average, atoms with a shorter half-life will decay sooner than atoms with longer half-lives.

Alpha Particles

The alpha particles making up alpha rays turned out to be made of two protons and two neutrons, in other words, a helium nucleus. They are sometimes written $^4_2\alpha$ to remind us that they have atomic number Z = 2 and mass number A = 4. When an unstable nucleus decays by alpha decay, an alpha particle is ejected from the nucleus. The alpha particle carries two protons and two neutrons away from the nucleus. Since the remaining nucleus has two fewer protons, its atomic number decreases by two, which means that it becomes a different element. In addition, the atomic mass number decreases by four, because two protons and two neutrons are removed.

Uranium is a good example of an element that decays by alpha emission. Uranium is a naturally occurring unstable element that was present in the clouds of gas and dust that collapsed to form the Earth. The most common isotope of uranium is ^{238}U. Because the half-life of uranium-238 is 4.5 billion years, there is still plenty of it around. Of all the uranium-238 that was present when the Earth was formed, only about half of it has decayed by now, meaning there is still half of it left. When ^{238}U decays, it does so by alpha emission. Thus, the mass number decreases by four from 238 to 234. In addition, the atomic number decreases from Z = 92 for uranium down to Z = 90, which is the atomic number of thorium. This means that the decay of uranium-238 proceeds as follows:

$$^{238}_{92}U \rightarrow {}^{234}_{90}Th + {}^{4}_{2}\alpha$$

A diagram of this decay is shown schematically in Figure 6.2.

Beta Decay

Another form of radioactive decay is beta emission. Beta decay occurs when a neutron in an atomic nucleus turns into a proton, emitting an electron and an **antineutrino**. The beta particle that

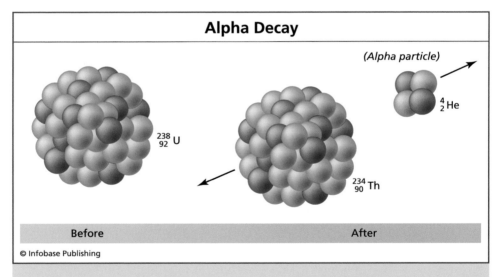

© Infobase Publishing

Figure 6.2 *Radioactive decay of a nucleus of uranium-238 by alpha emission. The alpha particle carries away two protons and two neutrons, changing the atomic number of the nucleus from 92 to 90, the atomic number of thorium (Th). The atomic mass number decreases by four as well, from 238 to 234.*

emerges from this reaction is the electron that comes flying out of the nucleus, leaving the atom entirely. Since one of the neutrons in the nucleus turns into a proton, after beta emission the atomic number goes up by one, changing the atom to the next one along in the periodic table. But the total number of protons plus neutrons does not change, so the mass number remains the same. For example, carbon-14 is the radioactive carbon isotope used for dating. It decays by beta emission, changing its atomic number from Z = 6 for carbon to Z = 7, which means it becomes nitrogen. But the mass number doesn't change. Thus we can write:

$$^{14}_{6}C \rightarrow \, ^{14}_{7}N + \beta^- + \bar{\nu}_e$$

where the β^- is just another way of representing an electron. The beta decay of $^{14}_{6}C$ into $^{14}_{7}N$ is shown in Figure 6.3.

Beta decay occurs if there are too many neutrons in the nucleus, because in the process one neutron is converted into a proton. But for nuclei with too many protons there is a similar decay mode called β^+ decay or **positron emission**. This is essentially the reverse of beta decay. In positron emission, a proton in the nucleus turns into a neutron and emits a **positron** and a **neutrino**. The positron is just like an electron, except that it carries a positive electric charge. The neutrino is both neutral and has a very tiny mass, so it is very difficult to detect. Since positron emission is characterized by a proton turning into a neutron, the atomic number of the nucleus decreases by one but the mass number stays the same. For example, the most common form of sodium is $^{23}_{11}Na$, which is stable. The isotope $^{22}_{11}Na$, however, is radioactive and decays by positron emission with a half-life of 2.6 years. When a nucleus of sodium-22 decays, it emits a positive beta particle, changing its atomic number from Z = 11 for sodium to Z = 10, which means it becomes neon. Since the mass number doesn't change, we are left with neon-22, which makes up about 9% of the naturally occurring neon. We can show this decay as a formula:

$$^{22}_{11}Na \rightarrow \, ^{22}_{10}Ne + \beta^+ + \nu_e$$

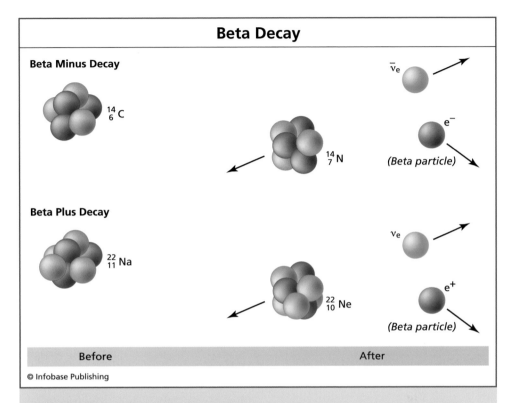

Figure 6.3 *Carbon-14 decays by emitting a negative beta particle (electron) and an antineutrino. This increases the atomic number by one, while leaving the mass number the same, yielding nitrogen-14 (top). Sodium-22 decays by emitting a positive beta particle (positron) and a neutrino. This decreases the atomic number by one, while leaving the mass number the same, yielding neon-22 (bottom).*

where the β^+ stands for the positron, which is sometimes also written e^+. The positive beta decay of ^{22}Na into ^{22}Ne is shown in the bottom panel of Figure 6.3.

The decay of a neutron into a proton that characterizes beta decay is caused by the weak nuclear force. Usually this force lives up to its name and is so weak that it doesn't have any noticeable effects. But when a neutron turns into a proton inside a nucleus, it is much easier to detect. Since the atomic number changes, the atom becomes a different element. Even though beta decays don't happen very often, when they do, they offer an important window into the functioning of this important, fundamental force.

Gamma Decay

It turns out that the particles that make up gamma rays are actually photons, the same particles that make up visible light. The photons in gamma rays, however, carry much more energy than the photons in visible light. Emission of gamma rays does not change either the mass number or the atomic number of the atom. Instead, it is just a release of extra energy in the nucleus. The extra energy is due to vibrations in the nucleus remaining after a previous radioactive decay. Figure 6.4 shows the nucleus of dysprosium-152 getting rid of excess rotational energy by the emission of a gamma ray.

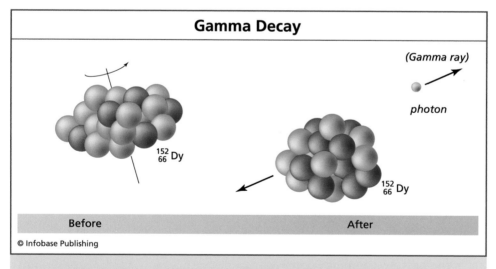

Figure 6.4 *The excess rotational energy of a dysprosium-152 nucleus is emitted in the form of a gamma ray. Neither the atomic number nor mass number changes due to gamma emission, so the final nucleus is still dysprosium-152.*

DANGERS OF RADIOACTIVITY

Radioactive decays often produce alpha particles, beta particles, or gamma rays that can disrupt the cells in the human body. Precautions must be taken in order to handle radioactive materials safely. Of course, this wasn't known initially, so the early scientists studying radioactivity didn't protect themselves at all. This led to sad consequences for the Curies and other scientists who studied radioactivity.

In the extreme case of very high radiation exposure, cells and organs can be destroyed quickly, resulting in a rapid and painful death. Radiation, however, can have more subtle effects. The high energy particles coming from radioactive decays can penetrate human cells and hit the DNA that makes up the cellular blueprints. Sometimes this results in a change in the DNA, called a mutation. Most of the time such mutations are harmless, but occasionally a mutation can lead to major changes in the behavior of the cell. The most common worry is that the mutation will lead to uncontrolled replication of the cell; in other words, the cell becomes cancerous.

Natural Sources of Radiation

There are many sources of naturally occurring radioactivity. All matter contains a small fraction of isotopes that are unstable and decay radioactively. So all of us are exposed to very low levels of radioactivity simply because we live on the Earth. In fact, a small fraction of all the carbon atoms in your body are the radioactive isotope ^{14}C. The small amount of radiation given off when they decay doesn't affect your body very much. In fact, the presence of this isotope can be useful for dating ancient remains.

Another natural source of radiation is cosmic rays. These are high-energy particles from outer space that happen to strike the Earth. Many of the cosmic rays are deflected by the Earth's magnetic field or stopped by the atmosphere, but some make it all the way to the ground. If you fly in an airplane there will be more cosmic rays that reach you because there is less atmosphere above you to act as a shield. But even so, the amount of radiation one gets from cosmic rays is usually not a cause for concern.

Radon, $_{86}$Rn, is a noble gas that is radioactive. It is produced naturally in the Earth's interior by the decay of heavier radioactive elements and gradually seeps out of the ground. Usually the amounts of radon from the ground are not dangerous. Sometimes, however, radon can be trapped in basements and remain at high levels that can be dangerous to the people living in the house. For this reason, people in areas known to have a significant amount of radon will have their basements tested to see whether the level of radon is too high.

Artificial Sources of Radiation

Radioactive materials are produced as the result of human activities. For example, nuclear power plants make use of nuclear decays to produce energy, as will be discussed in Chapter 7. The byproducts of such plants, however, contain highly radioactive materials. It is difficult to store such high concentrations of radioactive waste because there is always a danger that some might leak into the ground and contaminate the soil or water supplies.

Another source of radiation exposure is in the form of X-rays and other medical imaging techniques. While these procedures yield valuable information that help doctors diagnose diseases, there is also a small amount of risk from the radiation exposure. For this reason, X-ray imaging is only used when the benefits from the medical diagnosis outweigh the risks from radiation exposure.

APPLICATIONS OF RADIOACTIVITY

In addition to the dangers posed by radioactivity, it can also have many useful applications. We have already seen how Rutherford used beams of alpha particles in his discovery of the atomic nucleus. We also mentioned that the study of beta decay gives insight into the properties of the weak nuclear force. There are many other areas where sources of radioactivity can be used as powerful tools for learning about the world and even healing people.

Dating

As mentioned earlier, all living things contain radioactive isotopes in their bodies. This is a useful fact that can be exploited to determine the age of an ancient sample of organic material. Every animal or plant has a certain ratio of radioactive carbon, ^{14}C, to stable carbon, ^{12}C. Even though the ^{14}C gradually decays and disappears, while the organism is alive it is constantly replenishing the amount of ^{14}C in its body by absorbing carbon dioxide or eating other plants or animals. Thus the ratio of ^{14}C to ^{12}C remains constant while the organism is alive. After the organism dies, however, it stops eating and breathing, so the ^{14}C that decays is not replaced. This means that the ratio of ^{14}C to ^{12}C starts to decrease and keeps getting smaller with time. Therefore, a sample that has a smaller ratio of ^{14}C to ^{12}C will be older than one with a larger ratio. If the ratio is measured very carefully, accurate dates can be determined.

Medical Applications

Radioactivity can be beneficial to human health through its applications to medical technology. Radioactivity can be used to help in the treatment of cancer through radiation therapy. As mentioned above, intense radioactivity can disrupt the functioning of living cells by destroying the internal DNA blueprints used to rebuild the cell. Cancerous cells grow very rapidly and use their DNA more frequently than noncancerous cells. Therefore, radioactivity will harm the cancerous cells more than the healthy cells. By directing a radioactive dose at a tumor, doctors can destroy many of the cancerous cells. Unfortunately, the healthy cells that are near the tumor are also affected, but not quite as much as the cancerous cells. So radiation therapy is harmful to cancerous and noncancerous cells alike, but the goal is to focus the damage on the cancerous cells and damage them enough to stop the cancer from growing and spreading.

Another type of ray discovered in 1895 was the X-ray. X-rays are not associated with nuclear decay as are alpha, beta, and gamma rays. X-rays, however, are very similar to gamma rays and are often discussed together with radioactivity. X-rays are composed of particles of light—namely, photons—with energy higher than visible light, but lower energy than gamma rays. Because the X-rays have more energy than visible light, they can penetrate skin and muscle. They are stopped, however, by harder substances like bone. This allows X-rays to be used to take a picture of the bones inside a human body. To make a standard image, X-rays shine through the body from one direction and leave a shadow on photographic film on the other side of the body. More sophisticated imaging called computerized tomography or CT scans also rely on X-rays. In a CT scan, a very thin beam of X-rays is sent through a specific part of the body and a sensor records how many of the X-rays make it through the body. Then another beam is sent through nearby and at a slightly different angle, intersecting some of the same tissues. After making many measurements of this sort, a computer is used to reconstruct a three-dimensional image of the body.

CHAPTER 7

Nuclear Energy

THERE IS ONE PHYSICS EQUATION THAT NEARLY EVERYONE knows, but out of those millions of people only a small fraction really understand what the equation means. The equation is Albert Einstein's famous $E = mc^2$. This relatively simple formula relates energy, E, to mass, m, and the speed of light, $c = 299,792,458$ m/s. Einstein's formula indicates that mass is a form of energy. The formula, however, doesn't tell you how to actually go about converting mass into energy. That conversion most readily happens in the nuclei of atoms and is the subject of this chapter.

In the previous chapter, we discussed radioactivity in terms of the energy that is emitted from an unstable nucleus in the form of rays or particles. There are two more important processes that atomic nuclei can undergo, called fission and fusion, that are closely related to the radioactive decays discussed before.

Recall that isotopes are types of atoms that have the same number of protons but different numbers of neutrons. Most often, each element has a preferred number of neutrons, and nuclei with that number of neutrons are stable. If you add more neutrons or take some away, the nucleus usually becomes unstable and will break apart into smaller pieces that form the nuclei of new elements. **Fission** is the process by which a very large nucleus breaks up into two smaller nuclei. The sum of the masses of the smaller daughter nuclei is always slightly less than the mass of the original parent nucleus. Where did that extra mass go? It turns out that the tiny excess mass gets converted into energy. The amount of energy produced from the excess mass can be calculated from Einstein's formula $E = mc^2$.

On the other hand, **fusion** is the reverse process, by which two small nuclei come together to form one larger nucleus. In this case the sum of the masses of the original small nuclei is *greater* than the mass of the final nucleus. Again, this slight difference in mass turns into energy according to the relationship $E = mc^2$.

FISSION

Fission is the process by which an unstable nucleus breaks apart into two or more smaller nuclei. A good example is the radioactive isotope of uranium called $^{235}_{92}U$. Since the atomic number of uranium is 92, this means that $^{235}_{92}U$ has $235 - 92 = 143$ neutrons. $^{235}_{92}U$ is unstable and will decay by emitting an alpha particle:

$$^{235}_{92}U \rightarrow {}^{231}_{90}Th + {}^{4}_{2}\alpha$$

with a half-life of 700 million years. If an extra neutron is added to $^{235}_{92}U$, however, it will immediately undergo fission, breaking up into two smaller nuclei and also giving off several neutrons. This is shown schematically in Figure 7.1. For instance, one possible fission reaction is:

$$^{235}_{92}U + {}^{1}_{0}n \rightarrow {}^{140}_{54}Xe + {}^{94}_{38}Sr + 2({}^{1}_{0}n)$$

The neutron is indicated by the symbol $^{1}_{0}n$. In this example, the uranium-235 nucleus absorbs a neutron and breaks up into xenon-140 and strontium-94, and gives off two extra neutrons. We can

Nuclear Fission

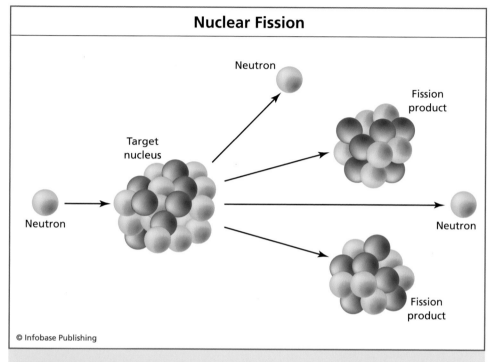

Neutron

Fission
product

Target
nucleus

Neutron

Neutron

Fission
product

© Infobase Publishing

Figure 7.1 *A target nucleus, like ^{235}U, absorbs a neutron and then breaks apart into two smaller nuclei (fission products) and several extra neutrons.*

check that this reaction makes sense by comparing the atomic numbers and mass numbers on both sides of the reaction. On the left side, the total mass number (total number of protons and neutrons) is 235 + 1 = 236, as given by adding the superscripts. On the right hand side the total mass number is 140 + 94 + 2 = 236, which matches the left side. To compare the numbers of protons, we can look at the subscripts that give the atomic number for each chemical symbol. On the left side of the equation we have uranium, which has an atomic number of 92. On the right side we have xenon with Z = 54 and strontium with Z = 38, for a total of 54 + 38 = 92 protons. Again, the left and right sides of the reaction match.

When a ^{235}U nucleus undergoes fission, it doesn't always turn into Xe and Sr. There are many other ways that it can split into two nuclei of roughly the same size. In all cases, however, the total mass of the daughter particles is less than the mass of the original ^{235}U nucleus, and that excess mass is converted into **kinetic energy** of the daughter particles. That means that the fission fragments go flying away at high speeds. These fragments then bump into nearby atoms, and their kinetic energy is converted into heat of the surrounding environment. This method of producing heat is the key to using fission reactions to produce energy in nuclear power plants.

APPLICATIONS OF FISSION REACTIONS

Most electrical power plants operate in the same way. They burn coal or natural gas to produce heat. The heat turns water into steam and the steam propels a large turbine. The turbine in turn rotates a large magnet that generates electric current. Nuclear power plants operate in exactly the same way, but instead of burning fuel they rely on a fission chain reaction to produce heat. Nuclear power plants take a very concentrated mixture of unstable atoms that are prone to decay by fission, like ^{235}U. As we saw above, when one ^{235}U nucleus absorbs a neutron, it splits into two smaller nuclei and also gives off some extra neutrons. Those neutrons can then be absorbed by another ^{235}U nucleus and trigger a fission, giving off more neutrons. In this way the reaction can continue, each fission giving off energy and neutrons that can in turn trigger new fissions, forming a chain reaction. If the chain reaction proceeds too quickly, it will release so much heat that it will melt whatever container is holding the uranium. By inserting **neutron absorbers** into the ^{235}U fuel, however, the extra neutrons emerging from each fission can be caught before they trigger more fissions, stopping the reaction. By carefully balancing the amount of fuel against the amount of neutron absorbers, nuclear power plants force the chain reaction to proceed slowly and give off a constant amount of heat. That heat is then used to convert water

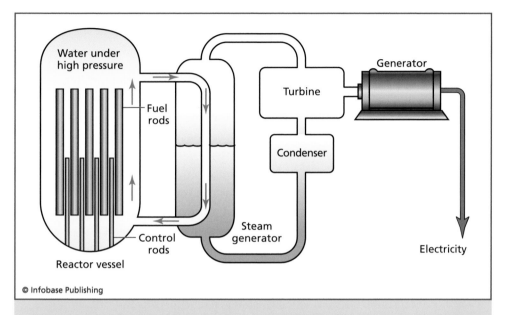

Figure 7.2 *A schematic of a nuclear power plant showing how the nuclear fuel heats up water to produce steam, which turns a turbine that powers an electrical generator. The steam is condensed back into water and is recycled through the plant.*

into steam, which turns the turbine that runs a generator and produces electricity, just like in coal- or gas-powered plants. This is shown schematically in Figure 7.2.

The presence of the neutron absorbers helps to control the chain reaction of fission decays. Without the neutron absorbers, the chain reaction can proceed very rapidly, giving off all the energy from the nuclear decays in a very short time. If the concentration of ^{235}U is high enough, much higher than that used in power plants, the chain reaction can lead to a huge explosion. This is the principle behind fission bombs. Besides producing electricity to power our houses, the energy released by atomic nuclei breaking apart can be used as a weapon to destroy buildings and kill people.

A Natural Fission Reactor

In the West African country of Gabon, there is a rich uranium deposit. Two billion years ago, the concentration of ^{235}U was high enough that a fission reaction was able to start and continue in a chain reaction for several hundred thousand years. Since the reaction stopped billions of years ago, however, how do we know that it occurred? One clue comes from the isotopic abundance of neodymium, $_{60}Nd$. Several isotopes of neodymium occur naturally, the two most prevalent being ^{142}Nd and ^{144}Nd. Neodymium isotopes are also present in the decay products of $^{235}_{92}U$ fission reactions. Uranium fission, however, produces very little ^{142}Nd but a lot of ^{143}Nd. Looking at the abundance of different isotopes of neodymium in a place called Oklo in Gabon, scientists found that there was very little ^{142}Nd and lots of ^{143}Nd. This is exactly what would be expected to result from a fission chain reaction. Thus the first working fission reactor on Earth was in West Africa, long before the emergence of human beings.

FUSION

Fusion is the reverse of fission. During nuclear fusion, two small nuclei come together and merge to form one larger nucleus. But as in fission, each fusion reaction gives off lots of excess energy.

A good example of fusion reactions is the merging of a hydrogen nucleus with a deuterium nucleus to form an isotope of helium. Deuterium (^2_1H or D) is a heavier isotope of hydrogen that has one neutron in addition to the single proton in hydrogen. Imagine trying to put the hydrogen and deuterium nuclei together. First, you would notice that the positive charges of the protons mean that the two nuclei will not want to be brought close together because of the repulsive nature of the electric force between like charges. If you use enough force to overcome the electrical repulsion, however, you can put the proton and deuterium nucleus together. The new nucleus has two protons and one neutron. The atomic number is $Z = 2$, which means you now have helium. Since there is only one neutron, the mass number is three, yielding ^{3}He, an isotope of helium that is slightly lighter than ^{4}He because it is missing a neutron. In practice, this reaction will occur if the temperature is high enough to overcome the electric repulsion between the protons.

Where is the temperature high enough for such fusion reactions to occur? One of the hottest places nearby is the sun, which is indeed powered by fusion reactions. The hydrogen in the center of the sun is being fused together to create helium nuclei, a process that also gives off lots of energy in the form of heat. Part of the reaction is the hydrogen-deuterium fusion described above.

APPLICATIONS OF FUSION REACTIONS

Fusion reactions can also be produced artificially on Earth. By making machines that reach extremely high temperatures and pressures, scientists have been able to produce fusion reactions in the lab. The hope is to eventually use fusion to run power plants to produce electricity in the same way that fission reactions are currently used. So far, however, the machines that produce fusion reactions consume far more energy than they produce, making fusion energy impractical. There would be many benefits from getting energy from fusion rather than fission or burning fossil fuels. Fusion energy would be relatively clean and safe. Therefore, scientists and engineers are still working hard to overcome the technical hurdles that prevent widespread use of fusion power. But it is a difficult challenge, and even though significant progress has been made in the last 30 years, it is not known when, if ever, fusion energy will be generating the electricity we use in our homes.

Fusion Weapons: The H-bomb

Just like fission reactions, fusion reactions can proceed rapidly enough to create a huge explosion. This is the principle behind the hydrogen-bomb or H-bomb. The destruction of the Japanese

Powering Stars

Stars are the pre-eminent example of fusion reactors. Fusion reactions in the core of the sun produce the energy that warms the Earth and makes life possible. All stars start out their lives by fusing protons together to form helium. In about 5 billion years, after all the hydrogen in the sun's core is used up, it will start to fuse helium nuclei together to form beryllium: $^4_2He + ^4_2He \rightarrow ^8_4Be$. But beryllium-8 is very unstable and breaks apart again almost immediately. If a third ^4_2He nucleus collides with the ^8_4Be before it decays, however, then those nuclei fuse together to form $^{12}_6C$. For stars that are at least four times the size of the sun, the fusion processes continue with heavier nuclei. Once the helium in the core is used up, the carbon undergoes fusion to produce oxygen, neon, sodium, and magnesium. Periods of neon fusion, oxygen fusion, and silicon fusion can all take place. There is a limit to the fusion process, however. One of the products of silicon fusion is iron, $_{26}Fe$. Iron nuclei cannot be combined to form a heavier nucleus; neither can they be broken up to form smaller nuclei. Iron nuclei are the most stable nuclei around. Thus, once a star has converted all its internal fuel to iron, the engine inside the star stops. Depending on how big the star was initially, this end can be in the quiet form of cooling off to become a white dwarf or it can be in the spectacular form of an enormous explosion called a supernova. Supernovae are very important because in the extremely hot environment of those explosions, more fusion reactions take place, producing heavy elements like mercury, lead, and uranium. All of the heavy elements found on Earth were produced in ancient supernova explosions.

cities of Hiroshima and Nagasaki during World War II demonstrated that fission bombs were capable of massive amounts of destruction. Nevertheless, scientists and governments in the U.S. and Soviet Union proceeded to develop bombs with 1,000 times more power by using fusion reactions in addition to fission reactions. In

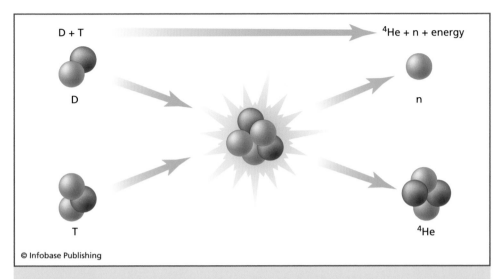

Figure 7.3 *Two isotopes of hydrogen, deuterium (D or ^2_1H) and tritium (T or ^3_1H), fuse to form a ^4_2He nucleus plus a neutron.*

an H-bomb, the fusion reaction between the hydrogen isotopes of deuterium and tritium, shown in Figure 7.3, is started by the explosion of a fission bomb that surrounds the hydrogen fuel. Even though the first fusion bomb was successfully tested in 1952, scientists are still working to develop a sustainable fusion reactor to generate power. It is unfortunate that the technology for building weapons capable of enormous destruction is so much easier to develop than the technology for extracting useful energy from fusion reactions.

CHAPTER 8

Elementary Particle Physics

I N AN ATOM, HIDDEN WITHIN THE CLOUD OF ELECTRONS IS the much smaller nucleus. Nuclei are extremely tiny, but they are made up of protons and neutrons that are smaller yet. Those protons and neutrons themselves are made out of even smaller quarks. Will this sequence of smaller and smaller constituents ever end? What is the smallest thing in the universe? The quest to answer these questions pushes scientific experiments to the extremes.

Probing smaller and smaller particles requires higher and higher energies. Producing such high energies requires bigger and bigger machines. It is ironic that the search for the smallest, most fundamental constituents of matter requires enormous detectors, amazingly high energies, and thousands of scientists. For example, the ATLAS detector, being built to look for the Higgs particle (described later in this chapter), is the size of a five-story building. There are 1,800 physicists working on this one, enormous experiment.

MATTER PARTICLES

Quarks

In the 1960s, it was discovered that protons and neutrons are in turn made up of smaller particles called quarks. The proton is made of two up quarks and one down quark. Since the up quark has an electric charge of +2/3 and the down quark has an electric charge of −1/3, the total charge of the proton is 2/3 + 2/3 − 1/3 = +1. On the other hand, the neutron has nearly the same mass as the proton but has zero electrical charge, so it stands to reason that the neutron is made up of one up quark and two down quarks: 2/3 − 1/3 − 1/3 = 0.

Protons and neutrons are held together in nuclei by the strong nuclear force. It turns out that the same force holds the three quarks together to make up a proton or a neutron. Just as the electrical force pulls opposite electrical charges together, the strong force pulls opposite "strong charges" together. Electric charges come in two types, positive and negative. But the strong charges come in *three* types. These three different charges are called colors, though they have nothing to do with light. The three charges can be thought of as red, green, and blue. Each type of quark can come in any of the three colors; for instance, there are red up quarks, blue up quarks, and green up quarks. The strong force always binds quarks together into colorless particles. Thus, the proton must be made up of one red, one green, and one blue quark. The same is true for the neutron. Particles like the proton and neutron that are made out of quarks are collectively known as **hadrons**.

Even though all you need to make protons and neutrons are up and down quarks, nature has provided yet more building blocks. Unusual particles had been observed as early as 1947 in the decay of cosmic ray particles. Since these decays were odd, they named the new particles "strange particles." When the idea of quarks arose in 1964, it was clear that these strange particles could be understood if there were a third quark besides the up and down quarks. Not surprisingly, this third quark was called the "strange quark." The strange quark has an electric charge of $-1/3$, making it just like the down quark except that it is a lot heavier. The strange quark wasn't the last discovery, however. Three more heavy quarks have been discovered. There is another negatively charged quark called the "bottom quark" that is even heavier than the strange quark. There are also two more quarks with electric charge $+2/3$ like the up quark, but much heavier. They are called the "charm quark" and the "top quark." These six quarks fit into three families, each family consisting of one quark with electric charge $+2/3$ and the other with electric charge $-1/3$. So far scientists haven't seen anything inside a quark, so we consider them elementary particles.

Leptons

There is another class of elementary particles besides the quarks. They are called **leptons**. One of the leptons is the familiar electron that is responsible for all the chemical interactions between atoms. A partner of the electron is the neutrino, which we encountered before in the discussion of beta decay. Just as there are three families of quarks, there are three families of leptons. Each lepton family consists of a negatively charged particle like the electron and a neutral, extremely light particle like the neutrino. The second lepton family contains the muon, which is a heavier version of the electron, and its partner, the muon neutrino. A yet heavier version of the electron is the tau, and it too has a companion, tau neutrino.

The charged leptons have electromagnetic interactions, but the neutrinos, being neutral, do not. None of the leptons feel the strong nuclear force at all. Leptons do feel the weak nuclear force, however. This means that the only way neutrinos can be observed is through their interactions with particle detectors via the weak nuclear force. This means that they are notoriously difficult to observe. In fact, they were some of the last elementary particles to have been directly detected. The electron neutrino was seen in 1956 and the muon neutrino was observed in 1962. But the first direct observation of the tau neutrino wasn't confirmed until July

Solar Neutrinos

The sun is a prodigious source of neutrinos. Most of the nuclear reactions taking place inside the sun emit neutrinos that go flying off into space. Some of the neutrinos fly towards the Earth. Because the neutrino interactions with other matter particles are so weak, most neutrinos don't notice the Earth and go flying right through its center and out the other side. In fact, every second roughly 60 billion neutrinos pass through every square centimeter of your body! But a very small number of neutrinos do interact in the Earth, so physicists have built enormous detectors to try to see them.

One example of such a detector is the Super-Kamiokande detector in Japan, shown in Figure 8.1. For many years the number of neutrinos detected arriving from the sun was about half the amount expected, based on the known nuclear reactions inside the sun. More detailed measurements make by Super-Kamiokande and other solar neutrino experiments recently solved this riddle. The answer was that the electron neutrinos produced in the sun turned into muon and tau neutrinos during their trip to the Earth. The muon and tau neutrinos are even harder to detect than electron neutrinos, which explains why earlier experiments hadn't seen enough neutrinos. The exciting implication of this solution is that neutrinos, long thought to be massless particles, must actually have a very small but nonzero mass.

Figure 8.1 *View inside Super-Kamiokande, a 50,000-ton tank of water located approximately 1 kilometer underground in Japan that detects neutrinos from the sun. The water acts as both the target for neutrinos and the detecting medium for byproducts of neutrino interactions.*

2000. It was detected at Fermilab, a powerful particle accelerator in Illinois.

FORCE PARTICLES

In Chapter 1, we discussed the four fundamental forces: gravity, electromagnetism, the weak nuclear force, and the strong nuclear force. Elementary matter particles like quarks and leptons interact by exchanging the different force carriers. For example, the photon is the particle that carries the electromagnetic force, so it is through the exchange of photons that a positive proton and negative electron are attracted to each other. Similarly, the strong nuclear force is transmitted by the exchange of particles called **gluons**. Though there is only one kind of photon, there are eight kinds of gluons. The weak nuclear force is transmitted by the exchange of particles called W bosons and Z bosons. These two particles are very heavy, so they are more difficult to exchange. This accounts for the weakness of the weak nuclear force. Gravity is not a very important force on the atomic or nuclear scale, but its force carrier has been given a name anyway: the **graviton**.

THE STANDARD MODEL

Together, these matter particles and force particles are the constituents of the **standard model of particle physics**, often simply called the standard model. The matter particles fit into three families, each family consisting of two quarks, one positive and one negative, and two leptons, one charged and the other neutral. All the atoms and material in our everyday lives is built out of the particles of the first family. The matter particles all interact by the exchange of force particles. The mathematical description of these interactions is given in the language of **quantum field theory**, of which quantum electrodynamics (QED) is a prime example.

This isn't quite the whole story. Each of the particles of the standard model has an **antiparticle** partner that is exactly the same except it has all the opposite electric and strong charges.

TABLE 8.1   Elementary Particles of the Standard Model*

Quarks	Up	Charm	Top	Photon	Force carriers
	Down	Strange	Bottom	Gluon	
Leptons	Electron neutrino	Muon neutrino	Tau neutrino	Z boson	
	Electron	Muon	Tau	W boson	
	I	II	III		
	Generations of Matter				

*The matter particles, quarks and leptons, come in three families. The force carriers mediate interactions between the matter particles.

Thus, a red up quark that has electric charge +2/3 has an antiparticle partner called an antiquark that has electric charge –2/3 and color charge anti-red. We already introduced the electron's antiparticle, the positron, when we discussed β⁺ decay in Chapter 6. The antiparticle of the positively charged W⁺ boson is the negatively charged W⁻ force particle. Antiparticles are produced in high-energy interactions, either in particle accelerators or by cosmic rays. Once produced, they don't last very long because they quickly run into one of their matter particles and annihilate in a burst of energy. One of the questions physicists are still trying to answer is why there is so much more matter in the universe than antimatter.

THE HIGGS PARTICLE

There is one final elementary particle that is important for the standard model but hasn't yet been observed in any experiment or detector. The Higgs particle is a neutral particle with a mass over 100 times that of a neutron. It plays a very important role

Common Words, Uncommon Meanings

It is surprising that so many common words are used to name the new particles and concepts that arise in elementary particle physics. For example, the six quarks are called up, down, charm, strange, top, and bottom, all words that are part of everyday speech. Of course, the names have nothing to do with the particles themselves. Scientists could call the six quarks anything. The use of common words, however, can be confusing to someone just learning about the subject. It certainly isn't obvious that a red bottom quark has nothing to do with colors or location. The precedent for unimaginative names goes back a long time, however. Recall the mysterious rays that were discovered in the 1890s. One type of ray was called an X-ray, where the X- was supposed to be a temporary name indicating that the makeup of the ray was unknown. The three types of radiation Becquerel discovered coming from uranium salts were called alpha, beta, and gamma rays, which are the first three letters of the Greek alphabet, equivalent to naming them A, B, and C rays. In more recent times, the unexpected particles observed in cosmic rays certainly were strange, so they were referred to as strange particles. By the time scientists finally figured out what X-rays, beta rays, and strange particles were, these temporary names had been used for so long that it was too hard to change, so the original, unimaginative names stuck. Unfortunately, using common words for specific, complex concepts can definitely lead to confusion. For example, there is *a* strong force of repulsion between an alpha particle and a gold nucleus. That repulsion, however, is not due to *the* strong force that is responsible for holding nuclei together. At least the Higgs particle has an interesting and unique name. It is named after Peter Higgs, one of the people who first proposed its existence.

in the standard model because it is by interacting with the Higgs particle that all the other elementary particles like quarks and leptons get their mass. In order to find the Higgs particle, physicists are constructing the highest energy particle accelerator ever

Figure 8.2 *The Large Hadron Collider (LHC) is being constructed at the European physics laboratory CERN on the border between France and Switzerland.*

built, the Large Hadron Collider (LHC). It is located at CERN, the European physics laboratory on the border between France and Switzerland (Figure 8.2). When the LHC turns on in 2008, it will accelerate protons to nearly the speed of light and then crash them into each other in the highest energy reactions produced since the beginning of the universe. The proton collisions will result in the production of many particles, perhaps including some Higgs particles.

EPILOGUE

In this book, we have only begun to explore the nature of matter. We have seen how the numerous types of materials around us are all made up of atoms consisting of positive nuclei surrounded by negatively charged electrons. We have also discussed how the interactions between the electrons in neighboring atoms account for the chemical bonding and chemical reactions that make each substance unique. There is much more to be learned, however. Atomic physics is the study of the detailed properties of atoms such as their energy levels. Condensed matter physics is the study of solids and their properties like electrical conduction. When we venture deeper into the atom, we encounter the tiny, positively charged nucleus composed of neutrons and protons. Changes in the nucleus result in radioactive decay, fission, or fusion. Not surprisingly, these interactions are the subject of nuclear physics. Elementary particle physics probes the smallest particles known, the quarks and leptons, searching for the ultimate constituents of matter.

GLOSSARY

ALKALI METALS   Highly reactive elements with a single valence electron; found in the first column of the periodic table.

ALKALINE EARTH METALS   Reactive elements with two valence electrons; found in the second column of the periodic table.

ALPHA PARTICLES   Nuclei of helium atoms; made of two protons and two neutrons; emitted from nuclei during alpha decay.

ALPHA RAYS   Weakly penetrating radiation from radioactive decay; can be stopped by a sheet of paper; consist of alpha particles.

ANGULAR MOMENTUM QUANTUM NUMBER   One of four quantum numbers that specify the location of an electron within an atom; represented by the symbol l; can take on values between 0 and $n - 1$.

ANTINEUTRINO   Antiparticle partner of the neutrino; a very light, neutral particle that is emitted along with an electron when a neutron turns into a proton during beta decay; an elementary lepton.

ANTIPARTICLE   Partner of a normal particle and identical in all respects except for having the opposite charges.

ATOMIC MASS NUMBER   Sum of the number of protons and neutrons in an atomic nucleus; represented by the symbol A; gives the approximate mass of an atom as measured in atomic mass units.

ATOMIC MASS UNIT   Measure of mass equal to 1.66×10^{-27} kg; represented by the symbol u.

ATOMIC NUMBER   Number of protons in an atomic nucleus; represented by the symbol Z.

ATOM   Basic constituent of an element; made of protons and neutrons in a tiny nucleus surrounded by a cloud of electrons.

BETA RAYS   Radiation emitted by radioactive nuclei; made up of electrons (or positrons in the case of positive beta rays).

BETA DECAY   Transformation of one nucleus into another when a neutron turns into a proton and emits an electron and antineutrino that leave the atom.

CATHODE RAYS   Rays emitted from metals subjected to high voltages; composed of electrons.

CHEMICAL FORMULA   Collection of chemical symbols describing which elements are contained in a compound; subscripts to the right denote the number of times each atom appears; ex: H_2O.

CHEMICAL REACTIONS   Combining or separating of chemical elements; interactions due to the interplay of electrons between atoms.

CHEMICAL SYMBOL   One or two letter abbreviation for each element—for example, H for hydrogen and Cu for copper.

COMPOUND   Material made up of more than one atom or element.

COVALENT BONDS   Attachment between two atoms that arises from the sharing of one or more electron pairs.

DOUBLE BOND   Covalent bond where two electron pairs are shared between two molecules; ex. $O=C=O$.

ELECTROMAGNETISM   Fundamental force responsible for the attraction between opposite electric charges; its force carrier is the photon.

ELECTRONEGATIVITY   Strength with which an atom pulls the electrons in a bond; determines whether electrons will be shared or exchanged between atoms.

ELECTRONS   Elementary particle called a lepton; carries a negative electromagnetic charge; surrounds the nucleus in atoms and determines the chemical properties of elements.

ELEMENTARY PARTICLES   Objects that cannot be broken up into anything smaller—for example, quarks and leptons.

ELEMENTS   Pure substances that are made up of only one type of atom; cannot be separated into simpler components using chemical reactions.

EXCLUSION PRINCIPLE   Rule that says no two electrons can have exactly the same quantum numbers.

FISSION   When a large atomic nucleus splits into two or more pieces, usually releasing additional neutrons and energy.

FORCES   Mechanism by which two particles interact with each other.

FUSION   Joining together of two or more smaller nuclei to form a larger atomic nucleus.

GAMMA RAYS   Radiation emitted by radioactive nuclei; made up of high-energy light particles.

GLUONS   Force carriers of the strong nuclear force.

GRAVITON   Force carrier for the gravitational force.

GRAVITY   Force that pulls massive objects together; keeps people on the Earth and the Earth in orbit around the sun.

HADRONS   Particles that are affected by the strong nuclear force—for example, quarks, protons, and neutrons.

HALF-LIFE   Time it takes for half of a radioactive sample to decay.

HALOGENS   Highly reactive elements in the second to last column of the periodic table with a single electron vacancy in their valence shell; very electronegative; seek to acquire electrons from other atoms.

HYDROGEN BOND   Weak intermolecular bond forming between a slightly positive hydrogen atom and a slightly negative atom on a different molecule.

IONIC BOND   Sticking together of two atoms after one has transferred its extra electrons to the other.

IONIZED   Atoms that have gained or lost electrons, leaving them with a net electrical charge.

ISOTOPES   Atoms with the same atomic number (number of protons) but different numbers of neutrons in their nuclei.

KINETIC ENERGY   Energy stored in the motion of objects.

LEPTONS   Elementary particles that do not feel the strong nuclear force—for example, electrons and neutrinos.

MAGNETIC QUANTUM NUMBER   One of four quantum numbers that specify the location of an electron within an atom; represented by the symbol m_l, can take on values between $-l$ and l.

MOLECULES   Most basic units of a substance that still have the properties of that original substance.

NEUTRINO   Very light, neutral particle that is emitted along with a positron when a proton turns into a neutron during positron emissions; an elementary lepton.

NEUTRON   Neutral constituent of the atomic nucleus with a mass of roughly 1 u; made up of two down quarks and one up quark.

NEUTRON ABSORBERS Substances like boron that capture neutrons without undergoing fission; important for controlling a fission chain reaction.

NEUTRON NUMBER Number of neutrons in an atomic nucleus; sometimes represented by the symbol N.

NOBLE GASES Elements found in the last column of the periodic table that have full valence shells and are thus very unreactive.

NUCLEUS Tiny, positively charged central region of the atom that contains most of its mass; made up of protons and neutrons.

ORBITAL The specific spatial location of an electron around an atom. Each orbital is specified by three numbers: n, l, and m_l.

PERIOD A row in the periodic table of elements.

PHOTON Smallest particle of light; carries a discrete amount of energy determined by the light's frequency.

PLUM PUDDING MODEL Early view of the atom in which negative electrons were stuck in a larger, smooth positive dough.

POLARIZED When electrical charge separates slightly in a molecule, leaving one side more negative and the other side more positive.

POSITRON Antiparticle partner of the electron; identical to the electron except that it carries positive electrical charge.

POSITRON EMISSION Radioactive decay whereby a proton in the nucleus turns into a neutron and emits a positron and a neutrino.

PRINCIPAL QUANTUM NUMBER One of four quantum numbers that specify the location of an electron within an atom; represented by the symbol n; can take on any integer value.

PROTON Positively charged constituent of the atomic nucleus with a mass of roughly 1 u; made up of two up quarks and one down quark.

QUANTUM FIELD THEORY Mathematical language in which the interactions of elementary particles are described.

QUANTUM NUMBERS Numbers that indicate where an electron is within an atom. The location of an electron is specified by the principal (n), angular momentum (l), magnetic(m_l), and spin quantum numbers (m_s).

QUARK   Elementary particle that feels the strong nuclear force; carries a fractional electric charge. Quarks exist in six varieties (up, down, charm, strange, top, bottom) and three "colors" (red, green, and blue).

REACTIVE   Eager to interact with other elements and either donate or steal valence electrons.

REDUCTIONISM   Attempt to understand a complex entity by looking at its smaller components.

RUTHERFORD MODEL   See solar system model.

SOLAR SYSTEM MODEL   More descriptive name for the Rutherford model of the atom, which features a dense, positive nucleus with electrons in orbit around it.

SPIN   A quantum mechanical property of electrons characterized by the quantum number $m_s = \pm 1/2$. It represents whether the electron's internal magnet is aligned with or opposite to an external magnetic field.

STANDARD MODEL OF PARTICLE PHYSICS   Description of matter particles (quarks and leptons) and their interactions via three fundamental forces, given in the language of quantum field theory.

STRONG NUCLEAR FORCE   Force that holds quarks together inside protons and neutrons and also holds protons and neutrons together in atomic nuclei; its force carriers are the gluons.

SUBSHELL   The subdivision of an electron shell, specified by the magnetic quantum number l. Subshells are also labeled by the letters s, p, d, and f.

VALENCE ELECTRONS   Electrons in the outermost energy level of an atom; responsible for the interactions between atoms.

VALENCE SHELL   Highest energy level of an atom that contains some electrons.

WEAK NUCLEAR FORCE   One of four fundamental forces; responsible for radioactive beta decay in atomic nuclei.

BIBLIOGRAPHY

Bryson, Bill. *A Short History of Nearly Everything.* New York: Broadway Books, 2004.

Freedman, Roger A., and William J. Kaufmann III. *Universe: Stars and Galaxies.* New York: W.H. Freeman, 2002.

Griffiths, David. *Introduction to Elementary Particles.* New York: John Wiley & Sons, 1987.

Halliday, David, Robert Resnick, and Kenneth S. Krane. *Physics, Vol. 2, Extended version*, 4th ed. New York: John Wiley & Sons, 1992.

Huheey, James E., Ellen A. Keiter, and Richard L. Keiter. *Inorganic Chemistry: Principles of Structure and Reactivity*, 4th ed. New York: Harper Collins College Publishers, 1993.

Ihde, Aaron J. *The Development of Modern Chemistry.* New York: Dover Publications, 1984.

Jaffe, Bernard. *Crucibles: The Story of Chemistry.* New York: Dover Publications, 1976.

Jolly, William L. *Modern Inorganic Chemistry*, 2nd ed. New York: McGraw-Hill, 1998.

Miessler, Gary L. and Donald A. Tarr. *Inorganic Chemistry*, 2nd ed. Upper Saddle River, NJ: Prentice Hall, 1999.

Serway, Raymond A., Clement J. Moses, and Curt A. Moyer. *Modern Physics.* Fort Worth, TX: Harcourt Brace Jovanovich College Publishers, 1989.

Wolfson, Richard. *Nuclear Choices: A Citizen's Guide to Nuclear Technology.* New York: McGraw-Hill Publishing, 1991.

FURTHER READING

Bryson, Bill. *A Short History of Nearly Everything.* New York: Broadway Books, 2004.

Cowan, George A. "A Natural Fission Reactor." *Scientific American* 235 (1976): 36–47.

Gamow, George. *The Great Physicists From Galileo to Einstein.* New York: Dover Publications, 1961.

Weinberg, Steven. *Dreams of a Final Theory.* New York: Pantheon Books, 1992.

Wolfson, Richard. *Nuclear Choices: A Citizen's Guide to Nuclear Technology.* New York: McGraw-Hill Publishing, 1991.

Web Sites

American Physical Society
http://www.aps.org/studentsandeducators/

The ATLAS Detector
http://atlas.ch

Contributions of 20th Century Women to Physics
http://cwp.library.ucla.edu

Eric Weisstein's World of Science
http://scienceworld.wolfram.com

The Large Hadron Collider
http://lhc.web.cern.ch/lhc/general/gen_info.htm

The Nobel Prize
http://nobelprize.org

The Particle Adventure: The Fundamentals of Matter and Force
http://particleadventure.org

The Periodic Table of the Elements
http://periodic.lanl.gov

Virtual Chemistry Club
http://www.chemistry.org/portal/a/c/s/1/acsdisplay.html?DOC=vc2\index.html

WebElements Periodic Table
http://www.webelements.com/webelements/scholar/index.html

PICTURE CREDITS

INDEX

A

accelerators, 90–92
alchemy, 63
alkali metals, 50
alkaline earth metals, 50
alpha particles, 22, 32, 66–67, 71
alpha rays, 64
Anaximines, 16
angular momentum quantum number (l), 39
antineutrinos, 67–68
antiparticles, 88–89
ATLAS detector, 84
atomic mass, 34–38
atomic mass units, defined, 31
atomic models
    Bohr model, 23–24, 26
    overview of, 20–21
    quantum mechanics and, 24–27
    Rutherford model, 22–23
atomic number (Z)
    beta decay and, 68
    defined, 29
    fusion and, 81
    nucleus and, 38
atoms
    chemical formulae and, 47–48
    construction of, 41–45
    gases and, 19
    in glass of water, 9
    Greeks and, 16–17
    overview of, 10–11
    size of, 14

B

baking, 17–19
balloons, 51

Becquerel, Henri, 64, 65
Berkeley, CA, 30
beryllium, 82
beta decay, 13, 67–70
beta particles, 71
beta rays, 64
Bohr atomic model, 23–24, 26
bonds. *See* chemical bonds
bosons, 88
bottom quarks, 86
breakfast cereal, 44

C

calcium, 49
cancer, 71, 73
carbon, 69, 73
carbon dioxide, 48
cathode rays, 20
cereals, 44
CERN, 91
Chadwick, James, 28
charge
    antiparticles and, 88–89
    electrons and, 42
    fusion and, 80–81
    ionic bonds and, 53–54
    ions and, 31–33
    polarization and, 56–57
    quarks and, 85–86
charm quarks, 86
chemical bonds
    chemical formulae and, 47–48
    covalent bonds, 54–56, 58–60
    electron sharing and, 52
    extra electrons and, 50
    filled, empty shells and, 48–50
    hydrogen bonds, 59, 60–62

ionic bonds, 52–54, 58–60
noble gases and, 51–52
overview of, 46–47
polarization and, 56–60
vacancies and, 50–51
chemical elements. *See*
elements
chemical formulae, overview of,
47–48
chemical properties, 34–39
chemical reactions, 19
chemical symbols, 29, 30
chlorine, 50–51
colors, strong charges and, 85
columns. See groups
compass needles, 13
compounds, elements and,
18–19
computerized tomography, 74
coolants, 51
cosmic rays, 71
covalent bonds, 54–56, 58–60
crystals, ionic bonds and, 54
CT scans, 74
Curie, Marie, 30, 64, 65
Curie, Pierre, 65

D
Dalton, John, 19, 20, 36
dangers of radioactivity, 71–72
dating techniques, 73
decay. *See* radioactivity
Democritus, 16–17
density, water temperature and,
59
detector construction, 84, 87
deuterium, 80–81
DNA
hydrogen bonds and, 61–62
as molecule, 10
radioactivity and, 71, 73

double bonds, 55–56
down quarks, 11, 85
dysprosium, 70

E
Einstein, Albert, 23–24, 30, 76
electrical power plants, 78
electromagnetism, 12–13, 88
electronegativity, 52, 56–58, 60
electronics, 51
electron neutrinos, 87
electrons
atom construction and, 41
atomic model development
and, 20–21
Bohr model and, 25
charge and, 32
chemical bonds and, 50
chemical properties and,
38–39
in glass of water, 9
interaction forces of,
14–15
leptons and, 86
numbering of, 40
orbitals and, 24–25
overview of, 11
quantum model and, 27
Rutherford model and, 23
spin and, 42
valence, 48–50
electron sharing, chemical
bonds and, 52
electron structure, periodic
table shape and, 43
elementary particle physics
elementary particles and,
11
force particles and, 88
Higgs particles and, 84,
89–92

matter particles and,
    85–88
  overview of, 84
  standard model and, 88–89
elements
  compounds and, 18–19
  defined, 17
  naming and symbols of, 30
energy, 41, 75–76
exclusion principle, 41

F

Ferme Générale, 18
Fermi, Enrico, 30
Fermilab, 88
fission, 76–80
fission bombs, 79
foil experiments, 22
fomulae, chemical, 47–48
forces
  fundamental, 12–13, 88
  particles and, 85–88
  quarks, electrons and,
    14–15
freezing, water density and, 59
French Revolution, 18
fructose, 48
fusion, 76, 80–83

G

Gabon, 80
gallium, 36
gamma decay, 70
gamma particles, 71
gamma rays, 64
gases, 19, 51–52
germanium, 36
gluons, 88, 89
gold, alchemy and, 63
gravitons, 88
gravity, 12–13

Greeks, matter and, 16–17
groups, electrons and, 49
gunpowder, 17

H

Hadron Collider, 91–92
hadrons, 85
half-life, 66
halogens, 50–51
H-bombs, 81–83
heat, 78
helium
  alpha particles and, 22, 66
  isotopes and ions of, 32
  as noble gas, 51–52
  stars and, 82
hemoglobin, 10
Higgs, Peter, 90
Higgs particles, 84, 89–92
Hiroshima, 82
hydrogen, 26, 80–81
hydrogen bombs, 81–83
hydrogen bonds, 59, 60–62
hypotheses, defined, 20

I

inert, defined, 51
ionic bonds, 52–54, 58–60
ionization, defined, 32
ions, 31–33, 47
isotopes, 29, 32

K

Kamiokande detector, 87
kinetic energy, 78

L

l (angular momentum quantum
    number), 39
Large Hadron Collider (LHC),
    91–92

Lavoisier, Antoine, 17–19
leptons, 86–88, 89

M

m (magnetic quantum number),
  39
magnetic fields, 51
magnetic quantum number (*m*),
  39
mass, Higgs particles and,
  89–91
mass extinctions, 75–76
mass number
  beta decay and, 68
  defined, 29–31
  fission and, 77
material, composition of, 14–15,
  85–88
medicine, 51, 72, 73–74
Meitner, Lise, 30
Mendeleyev, Dmitri, 30, 34–38
Meyer, Lothar, 38
microelectronics, 51
Miletus, 16
models, 20
molecules
  chemical formulae and, 48
  in glass of water, 7–9
  overview of, 10
muon neutrinos, 86, 87
muons, 86
mutations, 71

N

Nagasaki, 82
naming methods, 30, 90
neodymium, 80
neon, 82
neutrinos, 68, 86, 87
neutron absorbers, 79
neutron number, defined,
  29–31

neutrons
  atom construction and, 41
  beta decay and, 68
  fission and, 76–77
  in glass of water, 9
  nucleus stability and, 66
  overview of, 11, 28
  quarks and, 85
Newlands, John, 38
Newton, Isaac, 13
Nobel Prize, 42, 65
noble gases, 51–52
nuclear energy. *See also*
  radioactivity
  fission and, 76–80
  fusion and, 76, 80–83
  overview of, 75–76
nuclear forces. *See* strong
  nuclear forces; weak nuclear
  forces
nuclear physics, overview of,
  64–66
nuclear power plants, 72
nuclei
  atomic mass number and,
    29–30
  atomic mass units and, 31
  atomic number and, 29, 38
  fission and, 76
  in glass of water, 9
  Rutherford model and, 23
  size of, 14
nutrition, 44

O

Oklo, Gabon, 80
orbitals, 24–25, 39

P

particle accelerators, 90–92
particle physics, standard model
  of, 88–89

Pauli, Wolfgang, 42
periodic table of the elements, 34–38, 49
periods, 42–43, 49
photons
    electromagnetic force and, 88, 89
    gamma rays and, 70
    light and, 24
    X-rays and, 74
Pierrette, Marie-Anne, 18
Plato, matter and, 16
plum pudding model, 21
polarity, atomic bonding and, 57–58
polarization, 56–60
polonium, 65
positron emission, 68, 90
power plants, fission and, 78–80
principal quantum number, defined, 26, 39
protons
    atom construction and, 41
    atomic number and, 29, 66
    beta decay and, 67–68
    fission and, 77
    in glass of water, 9
    overview of, 11
    quarks and, 85

Q

quantum electrodynamics (QED), 25–26, 88
quantum field theory, 88
quantum levels, 39
quantum mechanics, 24–27
quantum numbers, 38–40
quarks
    antiparticles and, 90
    forces and, 88
    in glass of water, 9
    interaction forces of, 14–15
    overview of, 11, 85–86, 89

R

radioactivity. *See also* nuclear energy
    alpha particles and, 66–67
    applications of, 72–74
    beta decay and, 67–70
    dangers of, 71–72
    discovery of, 20, 64
    gamma decay and, 70
    nuclear physics and, 64–66
    overview of, 63–64
radium, 65, 66
radon, 72
raisin muffin model, 21
rays, atomic model development and, 20–21
reactions, chemical, 19
reactivity
    halogens and, 50–51
    noble gases and, 51–52
    of sodium, 56
    valence shells and, 49–50
reverse baking, 17–19
rows. *See* periods
Rutherford atomic model, 22–23

S

salt. *See* sodium chloride
scandium, 36
sharing of electrons, 54–56, 58–60
shells, filling of, 41, 48–50
sodium, beta decay and, 68–69
sodium chloride
    chemical formula of, 47–48
    electron sharing and, 60
    ionic bonds and, 52–53
    ions and, 31–32
    reactivity of, 46

solar system model, 22
spin, electrons and, 42
spinel, defined, 39–40
standard model of particle
    physics, 88–89
stars, fusion and, 82
steam power, 78–79
strange quarks, 85–86
strong charges, 85
strong nuclear forces
    as fundamental force,
        12–13
    gluons and, 88
    naming and, 90
    types of, 85
strontium, 76–77
subshells
    defined, 39
    electrons occupying, 40
    filling of, 41, 43–45
sugar, 18–19
sun, 81, 87
superconduction materials, 51
Super-Kamiokande detector, 87
supernovas, 82

T
tau, 86
tau neutrinos, 86–88
Thomson, J.J., 20–21
thorium, 67
top quarks, 86
triple bonds, 56
tumors, 73

U
up quarks, 11, 85
uranium
    alpha particles and, 66–67
    fission and, 76–78, 78–79
    Gabon and, 80

V
vacancies, 50–51
valence electrons, 48–50
valence shell, 48–50

W
water
    covalent bonds and, 54–56
    hydrogen bonds and, 60–61
    polarization and, 56–57
    properties of, 59
W bosons, 88, 89
weak nuclear forces
    bosons and, 88
    as fundamental force,
        12–13
    leptons and, 86
weapons, 79, 81–83
white dwarfs, 82

X
xenon, 76–77
X-rays, 72, 73–74, 90

Z
Z. *See* atomic number
Z bosons, 88, 89

ABOUT THE AUTHOR

DANIEL T. LARSON   grew up in St. Paul, Minnesota. He earned his undergraduate degree in physics and mathematics from Harvard University. Before heading off to graduate school, he spent another year at Harvard building prototype particle detectors for ATLAS, the world's largest science experiment. It will detect particles produced by the 5-mile diameter Large Hadron Collider (LHC) in Europe and help uncover the fundamental nature of matter. Daniel earned his Ph.D. in 2005 from the University of California, Berkeley, where he studied theoretical particle physics, with an emphasis on supersymmetry phenomenology. In his spare time, he enjoys training for various outdoor endurance events. He has completed an Ironman Triathlon and three 100-mile trail running races, along with countless shorter triathlons, marathons, and ultramarathons. Daniel is currently teaching physics part time at Harvard University.

ABOUT THE EDITOR

DAVID G. HAASE   is Professor of Physics and Director of The Science House at North Carolina State University. He earned a B.A. in physics and mathematics at Rice University and an M.A. and Ph.D. in physics at Duke University, where he was a J.B. Duke Fellow, and has been an active researcher in experimental low temperature and nuclear physics. Dr. Haase is the founding Director of The Science House (www.science-house.org), which annually serves more than 3,000 teachers and 20,000 students across North Carolina. He has co-authored more than 120 papers in experimental physics and in science education, and has co-edited one book of student learning activities and five volumes of Conference Proceedings on K-12 Outreach from University Science Departments. Dr. Haase has received the Distinguished Service Award of the North Carolina Science Teachers Association and was chosen 1990 Professor of the Year in the State of North Carolina by the Council for the Advancement and Support of Education (CASE).